Advanced Java Programming: Building Scalable Solutions

Master Java for Complex System Design and High-Performance Applications

Greyson Chesterfield

COPYRIGHT

DISCLAIMER

The information provided in this book is for general informational purposes only. All content in this book reflects the author's views and is based on their research, knowledge, and experiences. The author and publisher make no representations or warranties of any kind concerning the completeness, accuracy, reliability, suitability, or availability of the information contained herein.

This book is not intended to be a substitute for professional advice, diagnosis, or treatment. Readers should seek professional advice for any specific concerns or conditions. The author and publisher disclaim any liability or responsibility for any direct, indirect, incidental, or consequential loss or damage arising from the use of the information contained in this book.

Contents

Introduction: The Path to Advanced Java Mastery 8

    Purpose of the Book...9

    Who This Book is For..11

    What Readers Will Gain 13

    A Roadmap to Success in Advanced Java Development............................17

Chapter 1: Concurrency and Multithreading Essentials............20

    Java's Concurrency Model 20

    Thread Management and Pooling...23

    Handling Concurrency Issues: Deadlocks, Race Conditions, and Thread
    Safety 25

    Real-World Application: Optimizing a Web Server for High Traffic 28

    Benefits of Concurrency in High-Performance Applications.....................31

    Conclusion 32

Chapter 2: Memory Management and Optimization.................34

    Java's Memory Model 34

    Garbage Collection (GC) 36

    Techniques for Managing Memory Efficiently 39

    Example: Memory Optimization for Data-Intensive Applications..............42

    Conclusion 47

Chapter 3: Advanced Java Generics and Functional
Programming 48

    In-Depth Use of Java Generics 49

    Leveraging Functional Programming with Java 8+....................................54

    Streams API for Data Processing...56

    Scenario: Data Processing in Parallel with Streams and Lambdas..............59

    Conclusion 62

Chapter 4: Data Structures and Algorithms for High Performance
....64

    Optimal Data Structure Choices for Specific Applications 65

    Implementing Custom Data Structures..68

Algorithm Optimizations 72

Example: Creating a High-Speed Cache for Real-Time Data Access 74

Conclusion 80

Chapter 5: Advanced Exception Handling and Logging...........81

Robust Error Handling Strategies for Enterprise Applications...................81

Best Practices for Logging and Monitoring Application Health 86

Practical Case: Logging and Error Handling in a Microservices Setup 91

Conclusion 97

Chapter 6: Distributed Computing Fundamentals....................100

Basics of Distributed Systems 101

Java Support for Distributed Computing...103

Challenges and Strategies for Building Distributed Java Applications.....110

Case Study: A Load-Balanced Storage System 112

Conclusion 116

Chapter 7: Microservices Architecture with Java 117

Core Principles of Microservices Architecture...118

Using Spring Boot for Microservice Design 121

Managing Inter-Service Communication and Data Consistency...............125

Example: Scalable User Authentication Microservice 127

Conclusion 131

Chapter 8: Design Patterns for Scalable Java Applications 133

Key Design Patterns for Scalable Applications..133

Design Patterns for Distributed Systems 138

Design Patterns for Event-Driven Architecture..141

Scenario: Implementing the Observer Pattern for Event-Driven
Notifications..143

Chapter 9: Event-Driven and Reactive Programming.............149

Principles of Reactive Programming 149

Introduction to Project Reactor and RxJava 151

Creating Responsive, Resilient Applications with Non-Blocking I/O 153

Practical Example: Real-Time Stock Trading Application 156

Conclusion 162

Chapter 10: Performance Tuning and Optimization 164

Profiling Tools for Identifying Bottlenecks...............................164

Techniques for Code Efficiency 167

Scenario: Optimizing a High-Throughput Data Pipeline............172

Conclusion 178

Chapter 11: Advanced Java I/O for High Performance............180

Java NIO and Asynchronous Data Processing............................181

Memory-Mapped Files, File Channels, and Streaming Optimizations......187

Example: Efficient I/O for Real-Time Messaging Application.................192

Conclusion 196

Chapter 12: Serialization and Deserialization in Java..............197

Serialization Techniques for Optimized Data Transfer 198

Using Protocol Buffers, Avro, and Custom Serialization in Practice........206

Case Study: Data Serialization for High-Performance APIs 207

Conclusion 212

Chapter 13: Multi-Platform Java Development 213

Developing Java Applications Across Desktop, Web, and Mobile Platforms
....213

Tools for Cross-Platform Compatibility 220

Example: Building a Cross-Platform Mobile and Desktop Application ...222

Conclusion 231

Chapter 14: Java for Big Data and Machine Learning 233

Integrating Java with Big Data Tools 233

Building and Deploying Machine Learning Models in Java Applications239

Case Study: Recommendation System for an E-Commerce Platform.......244

Conclusion 248

Chapter 15: Dependency Injection and Inversion of Control...251

Dependency Injection Principles and Benefits for Scalable Systems........251

Using Spring's IoC Container for Creating Modular Applications...........257

Example: Modular Architecture for an Enterprise Java Application.........262

Conclusion 269

Chapter 16: Continuous Integration and Deployment (CI/CD)271

Setting Up CI/CD Pipelines with Jenkins, GitLab CI, and GitHub Actions
....271

Automated Testing and Deployment for Scalable Applications...............280

Practical Workflow: CI/CD for a High-Availability Microservices Setup282

Conclusion 287

Chapter 17: Testing and Debugging Strategies 289

Test-Driven Development (TDD) and Behavior-Driven Development
(BDD) 289

Advanced Testing Techniques with JUnit, Mockito, and Integration Testing
....294

Scenario: Testing a Complex Distributed System 300

Conclusion 306

Chapter 18: Security Best Practices in Java Applications........308

Implementing Security Best Practices: Data Protection, Secure APIs, and
Authentication..308

Java Security Features and Secure Coding Principles 316

Example: Secure Login and Payment Processing in an E-Commerce
Platform..319

Conclusion 325

Chapter 19: Java in Cloud Computing and Serverless
Environments...328

Deploying Java Applications on AWS, Azure, and Google Cloud 329

Cloud-Native Design, Serverless Functions, and Containerization...........334

Example: Serverless Java Application for Real-Time Image Processing..339

Conclusion 345

Chapter 20: Java for IoT and Edge Computing.........................346

Building Low-Latency Java Applications for IoT and Edge Devices 346

Integrating Java in Resource-Constrained Environments.........................350

Scenario: Real-Time Monitoring System for IoT Sensors 353

Conclusion 362

Chapter 21: Future Trends in Java Development 363

Emerging Trends and Upcoming Features 364

Java's Evolving Role in Areas Like Blockchain and AI 369

Final Thoughts: Encouraging Readers to Stay Adaptive and Continue
Learning 373

Conclusion 376

Conclusion: Continuing the Journey 378

Recap of Core Principles Learned and Their Applications 378

Final Tips for Implementing Java Principles in Your Own Projects 383

Future Outlook on Java's Place in Tech and Advice for Staying Up-to-Date
....385

Final Words...389

Introduction: The Path to Advanced Java Mastery

Java has long been one of the most trusted languages in the software development world, known for its portability, robustness, and strong community support. Over the decades, Java has continued to adapt to new technology trends and has maintained its status as a critical language for high-performance applications, scalable architectures, and enterprise-grade solutions. This book, *Advanced Java Programming: Building Scalable Solutions – Master Java for Complex System Design and High-Performance Applications*, is designed to provide a comprehensive journey through advanced Java programming, focusing on mastering complex system design, concurrency, distributed computing, and performance tuning—all necessary skills for building scalable, resilient, and modern Java applications.

Purpose of the Book

This book serves as a guide for Java developers who are looking to go beyond basic knowledge and dive into advanced topics that power scalable, high-performance systems. Today's software landscape demands applications that can handle vast amounts of data, scale seamlessly under heavy loads, and perform optimally across various devices and networks. Building such systems requires deep expertise in Java's advanced capabilities, and this book provides a structured roadmap to acquire that expertise.

Here are the main goals of the book:

1. **Master Advanced Java Fundamentals**: While basic Java is sufficient for small to medium projects, building large-scale applications demands an in-depth understanding of Java's concurrency model, memory management, advanced data structures, and optimizations. These topics form the core foundation of high-performance programming, and we'll dive deep into each area.

2. **Design for Scalability and Performance**: Scalability is the ability of a system to handle increasing loads without compromising performance. This book will guide you through the principles of designing Java applications that can scale, with an emphasis on architecture, optimized data handling, and the use of frameworks that support distributed systems and microservices.

3. **Understand Distributed Computing and Microservices**: Modern Java applications often involve multiple distributed components that

must work together seamlessly. This book will introduce you to the tools and patterns required for building and managing microservices in Java, leveraging frameworks like Spring Boot and cloud-native tools to achieve resilience and modularity.

4. **Explore Modern Integrations and Emerging Technologies**: Java is no longer confined to traditional desktop or server environments; it now plays a key role in cloud computing, big data processing, machine learning, and the Internet of Things (IoT). This book will provide insights into how Java integrates with these cutting-edge technologies, enabling you to stay competitive in the rapidly evolving tech landscape.

5. **Focus on Real-World Applications and Performance Tuning**: Understanding advanced concepts is important, but it's equally critical to know how to apply them in real-world scenarios. This book emphasizes practical application, with hands-on examples and scenarios that mirror the challenges faced by Java developers working on enterprise-level systems.

With these goals in mind, this book is structured to provide both theoretical and practical knowledge. Each chapter will include real-world examples, case studies, and performance-focused code implementations to give you a strong foundation in advanced Java topics. By the end, you'll have a thorough understanding of the techniques necessary to build robust, scalable, and high-performance applications.

Who This Book is For

This book is intended for developers who already have a solid understanding of Java fundamentals and are ready to level up their skills. You may be:

- **A Mid-Level Java Developer**: If you're an intermediate Java programmer who has worked with object-oriented programming, built a few Java applications, and is familiar with basic Java libraries, this book will help you bridge the gap to advanced topics. It will guide you through core topics like concurrency, distributed computing, and modern Java frameworks that are essential for high-performance applications.

- **A Senior Java Developer**: Even if you're an experienced Java developer, this book covers a range of advanced topics that can deepen your expertise. We'll explore memory management techniques, custom data structures, best practices for distributed systems, and real-world use cases that go beyond typical Java applications. Additionally, this book will serve as a reference for mastering performance tuning, resilience, and scalability techniques.

- **A Software Architect or Technical Lead**: For technical leads or software architects, this book provides essential knowledge for making informed architectural decisions. By understanding the intricacies of Java's performance optimizations, memory management, and concurrency models, you'll be better equipped to design and oversee the development of scalable, resilient applications.

- **An Enthusiast in Modern Java and Emerging Tech**: If you're passionate about exploring how Java fits into the latest technology trends, this book covers topics that go beyond the basics, including cloud computing, big data, IoT, and machine learning. Each of these topics will be explored through Java's ecosystem, equipping you with a broader understanding of Java's role in modern software development.

This book is designed with a focus on readability, real-world examples, and practical application. If you find yourself searching for more efficient ways to handle complex requirements, this book will offer actionable insights that can make a difference in your projects. We will strive to avoid jargon and instead focus on explaining advanced concepts in a way that's both approachable and deeply informative.

What Readers Will Gain

In today's software landscape, building high-performance, scalable applications is a necessity. This book provides readers with a structured path to mastering advanced Java skills, including:

1. **Concurrency and Multithreading Mastery**: Java's concurrency capabilities allow applications to perform multiple tasks simultaneously, improving efficiency and responsiveness. In this book, you'll learn about thread management, thread pooling, and the techniques for preventing common concurrency issues like deadlocks and race conditions. You'll also explore the latest advancements in reactive programming and non-blocking I/O, using frameworks like Project Reactor and RxJava.

2. **Advanced Memory Management and Performance Optimization**: Effective memory management is crucial for high-performance applications, especially in data-intensive environments. This book will cover Java's memory model, garbage collection mechanisms, and techniques for optimizing memory usage. By understanding how to manage memory efficiently, you'll be able to design applications that perform optimally under heavy loads.

3. **Scalable System Design with Microservices**: The microservices architecture has become a popular choice for building modular and scalable applications. This book will provide a comprehensive overview of microservices principles, the role of frameworks like Spring Boot, and strategies for managing inter-service communication and data consistency. You'll also explore best practices for deploying microservices in cloud environments, achieving scalability, and improving fault tolerance.

4. **Distributed Computing Fundamentals**: Java has a strong ecosystem for distributed computing, including tools like RMI (Remote Method Invocation), gRPC, and message brokers. This book will guide you through building distributed Java applications, handling network communication, and managing distributed data. By understanding the principles of distributed computing, you'll be able to create systems that handle large amounts of data and traffic efficiently.

5. **Real-World Performance Tuning Techniques**: Performance tuning is a skill that distinguishes high-performance applications from average ones. In this book, you'll learn to identify bottlenecks, use profiling tools, and optimize code for speed and efficiency. Real-world scenarios will demonstrate how to apply performance tuning techniques, ensuring that

your applications are responsive, fast, and ready for production use.

6. **Integrating Java with Modern Technologies**: Java's relevance has extended into new fields such as cloud computing, big data, machine learning, and IoT. This book will provide an introduction to using Java in these areas, along with examples of real-world applications. You'll learn to use cloud platforms, data-processing tools, and machine learning libraries to build modern, versatile applications that remain competitive in today's technology landscape.

7. **Building and Maintaining Resilient Systems**: Resilience is the ability of a system to handle failures gracefully and continue operating under challenging conditions. This book will introduce you to best practices for building resilient systems, including techniques for handling exceptions, monitoring performance, and setting up fallbacks. You'll also learn how to implement fault-tolerant designs with tools like Netflix's Hystrix and Spring Cloud.

8. **Security Best Practices in Java Development**: In today's digital landscape, security is a top priority. This book includes chapters on securing Java applications, with topics covering data protection, secure API calls, authentication, and authorization. By following security best

practices, you'll be equipped to build systems that are robust against common vulnerabilities.

9. **Future-Proofing Your Java Skills**: The technology landscape is constantly evolving, and staying up-to-date with Java's latest features and trends is essential for remaining competitive. This book will highlight emerging trends in Java development, including Project Loom for lightweight concurrency, GraalVM for enhanced performance, and Java's role in serverless computing and containerization.

A Roadmap to Success in Advanced Java Development

This book is structured to guide you through each of these topics step-by-step, from foundational knowledge to complex system design. Each chapter includes practical examples, code snippets, and exercises to reinforce learning, ensuring that you gain both theoretical understanding and practical experience. By working through this book, you'll acquire a complete toolkit for tackling the challenges of advanced Java development, enabling you to design and build applications that are scalable, resilient, and ready for production.

As you progress through this book, you'll encounter challenges that push your Java skills to new levels. Advanced Java development requires not just understanding of the language, but also a mindset for problem-solving and optimization. Whether you're improving the performance of an application, designing a fault-tolerant system, or integrating with modern technologies, each chapter will provide the knowledge and insights needed to overcome these challenges.

Let's embark on this journey together. Through dedication and practice, you'll gain the expertise required to build Java applications that can handle the demands of today's most challenging software environments. By the end of this book, you'll be equipped to master the world of advanced Java programming and build scalable, high-performance applications with confidence.

Part 1
Advanced Core
Concepts in Java

Chapter 1: Concurrency and Multithreading Essentials

Concurrency and multithreading are foundational concepts in advanced Java programming, essential for building applications that perform multiple tasks simultaneously, maximize CPU usage, and maintain responsiveness under high load. In today's world of high-performance, multi-core processors, a deep understanding of concurrency and multithreading is crucial for developing scalable Java applications. This chapter delves into Java's concurrency model, explains effective thread management, highlights key issues like deadlocks and race conditions, and demonstrates these principles through a real-world application: optimizing a web server for high traffic.

Java's Concurrency Model

Concurrency refers to the ability of a program to manage multiple tasks at once, while multithreading is one way to achieve concurrency by running multiple threads simultaneously. Java's concurrency model supports parallelism and efficient task execution, enabling applications to run faster and make better use of system resources.

The Basics of Threads and Processes

In Java, a thread is a small unit of execution within a process. Each Java application runs as a process on the operating system, and each process may contain multiple threads. Java supports multithreading by providing the Thread class and the Runnable interface, allowing developers to create, start, and control threads.

- **Process**: An independent program in execution, with its own memory space and resources.

- **Thread**: A smaller unit of execution within a process, sharing the same memory and resources as other threads in the same process.

Multithreading allows Java programs to perform multiple tasks in parallel, which is essential for applications that handle intensive tasks like data processing, real-time analytics, or high-traffic web services.

Java Concurrency API and the java.util.concurrent Package

Java introduced the java.util.concurrent package in Java 5 to improve support for concurrency, providing a rich set of classes for managing threads, handling concurrency issues, and optimizing task execution. This package includes:

- **Executor Framework**: Manages thread pools and task execution without directly managing threads.

- **Concurrent Data Structures**: Such as ConcurrentHashMap, CopyOnWriteArrayList, and BlockingQueue, which are optimized for concurrent access.

- **Synchronization Utilities**: Including ReentrantLock, CountDownLatch, Semaphore, and CyclicBarrier for managing thread coordination.

- **Atomic Variables**: Classes like AtomicInteger, AtomicBoolean, etc., for atomic operations on variables without explicit synchronization.

The java.util.concurrent package simplifies thread management, reduces the likelihood of concurrency issues, and improves overall application performance.

Thread Management and Pooling

Creating a new thread for every task can be inefficient, as starting and stopping threads consumes CPU time and memory. In high-load environments, this can lead to resource exhaustion and poor performance. Thread pooling is a technique that mitigates these issues by reusing a fixed number of threads to execute multiple tasks, thereby reducing overhead and improving efficiency.

The Executor Framework

The Java Executor Framework, part of java.util.concurrent, simplifies thread management by abstracting the creation, execution, and termination of threads. It offers several classes for thread pooling, including ExecutorService, ScheduledExecutorService, and ForkJoinPool.

1. **ExecutorService**: This interface provides a way to manage and control the lifecycle of tasks. The most common implementation is ThreadPoolExecutor, which allows for customized thread pools.

2. **ScheduledExecutorService**: Allows tasks to be scheduled to run after a delay or at fixed intervals.

3. **ForkJoinPool**: Designed for parallelizable tasks, the ForkJoinPool divides tasks into smaller subtasks and executes them in parallel.

Creating a Thread Pool

A thread pool is a group of pre-created worker threads that are managed by an Executor. When a task is submitted, it is assigned to an available thread in the pool, and if no threads are available, the task waits in a queue until a thread becomes free.

```
ExecutorService executor =
Executors.newFixedThreadPool(10);

for (int i = 0; i < 100; i++) {

    executor.submit(() -> {

        // Task to be executed by the thread pool

        System.out.println("Executing task in thread: " +
Thread.currentThread().getName());

    });

}

executor.shutdown();
```

In this example, a fixed thread pool with 10 threads is created, and 100 tasks are submitted for execution. By reusing threads, we reduce overhead and improve application performance, especially for high-traffic systems.

Handling Concurrency Issues: Deadlocks, Race Conditions, and Thread Safety

While concurrency offers many benefits, it also introduces potential issues. Common concurrency challenges include deadlocks, race conditions, and ensuring thread safety.

Deadlocks

A deadlock occurs when two or more threads are waiting for each other to release resources, resulting in a standstill where no progress is made. Deadlocks can severely impact application performance, especially in high-traffic environments.

Example of Deadlock: Consider two threads, Thread A and Thread B, where:

- Thread A holds Lock 1 and waits for Lock 2.

- Thread B holds Lock 2 and waits for Lock 1.

Both threads are now in a deadlock, as each is waiting for a resource held by the other.

Avoiding Deadlocks: To avoid deadlocks, consider:

- **Ordering Locks**: Establish a consistent lock order so threads acquire resources in the same order.

- **Timeouts**: Use timeouts when attempting to acquire locks, so threads don't wait indefinitely.

- **Avoid Nested Locks**: Minimize or avoid situations where multiple locks are held at the same time.

Race Conditions

A race condition occurs when two or more threads modify a shared resource simultaneously, leading to unpredictable results. For instance, if two threads increment the same variable at the same time, the final value may be incorrect.

Avoiding Race Conditions:

- **Synchronization**: Use the synchronized keyword to ensure only one thread accesses a critical section of code at a time.

- **Atomic Variables**: Use atomic variables, such as AtomicInteger, for operations that must be thread-safe without explicit synchronization.

Thread Safety

Thread safety ensures that a piece of code or data structure functions correctly when accessed by multiple threads simultaneously. In Java, synchronization and atomic operations can help maintain thread safety.

Example of Thread-Safe Counter Using AtomicInteger:

```java
import java.util.concurrent.atomic.AtomicInteger;

public class ThreadSafeCounter {
    private AtomicInteger counter = new
AtomicInteger(0);

    public void increment() {
        counter.incrementAndGet();
    }

    public int getCounter() {
        return counter.get();
    }
}
```

Here, AtomicInteger ensures that the increment operation is thread-safe, avoiding the need for explicit synchronization and reducing overhead.

Real-World Application: Optimizing a Web Server for High Traffic

Let's apply these concurrency principles to a real-world scenario: optimizing a web server to handle high traffic efficiently. A web server must process multiple requests concurrently, ensuring fast response times even during peak traffic.

Problem Statement

Consider a web server that serves hundreds of thousands of requests per minute. With a traditional approach, each request would require a new thread, leading to high overhead and resource exhaustion as the server scales. Using a thread pool and managing concurrency effectively can help handle large volumes of requests efficiently.

Solution: Implementing a Thread Pool and Concurrency Controls

1. **Setting Up a Thread Pool**:

    o Instead of creating a new thread for each request, we use a fixed thread pool to handle incoming requests.

    o A thread pool allows us to control the maximum number of concurrent threads, reducing overhead and ensuring consistent performance.

```java
import java.util.concurrent.ExecutorService;

import java.util.concurrent.Executors;


public class WebServer {
    private final ExecutorService executor =
    Executors.newFixedThreadPool(50);

    public void handleRequest(Runnable request) {
        executor.submit(request);
    }

    public void shutdown() {
        executor.shutdown();
    }
}
```

In this example, the WebServer class uses a fixed thread pool of 50 threads to handle requests. Incoming requests are submitted to the thread pool, ensuring that only a limited number of threads are active at any time, improving server performance and stability.

2. **Handling Concurrent Data Access**:

- A web server may need to manage shared resources, such as a database connection pool or an in-memory cache.

- By using synchronized blocks or concurrent data structures, we can ensure thread safety for shared resources, preventing issues like race conditions.

3. **Using Non-Blocking I/O**:

- In addition to thread pooling, the server can use non-blocking I/O (Java NIO) to handle requests without blocking threads unnecessarily.

- Non-blocking I/O enables threads to perform other tasks while waiting for data, further improving server responsiveness and throughput.

4. **Implementing Timeout and Graceful Shutdown**:

- To avoid long waits and potential deadlocks, implement timeouts when acquiring resources or processing requests.

- When the server shuts down, ensure that the thread pool is terminated gracefully to allow active threads to complete their tasks.

Benefits of Concurrency in High-Performance Applications

Effective use of concurrency and multithreading allows high-performance applications to:

- **Increase Throughput**: By handling multiple tasks simultaneously, applications can process more requests or tasks in less time.

- **Improve Responsiveness**: Applications that use multithreading can stay responsive to users, even when handling heavy workloads.

- **Optimize Resource Utilization**: Thread pools and non-blocking I/O make efficient use of system resources, minimizing idle time and reducing overhead.

- **Enhance Scalability**: Applications that handle concurrency effectively can scale to accommodate higher loads, making them suitable for enterprise and cloud environments.

Conclusion

Concurrency and multithreading are essential skills for Java developers aiming to build high-performance, scalable applications. By understanding Java's concurrency model, thread management, and pooling techniques, developers can create efficient applications that handle multiple tasks simultaneously, making the most of today's multi-core processors. Moreover, awareness of potential concurrency issues like deadlocks, race conditions, and thread safety is crucial for developing robust, reliable code.

In this chapter, we explored the fundamentals of concurrency in Java, discussed techniques for managing threads effectively, and demonstrated these concepts through a practical example of optimizing a web server for high traffic. These principles are foundational for advanced Java programming, and mastering them will empower you to build applications that perform well under real-world conditions.

As we move forward in this book, we'll build on these concepts to tackle more complex topics, including distributed computing, scalability, and resilience, equipping you with the skills to design and implement Java applications that are truly ready for enterprise demands.

Chapter 2: Memory Management and Optimization

Memory management is fundamental to building efficient and high-performance Java applications, particularly in data-intensive or resource-constrained environments. Understanding Java's memory model, garbage collection mechanisms, and techniques for optimizing memory usage is crucial for developing scalable and stable software. This chapter explores Java's memory model, offers best practices for memory management, and provides an example of memory optimization for data-intensive applications.

Java's Memory Model

Java's memory model defines how Java applications allocate, manage, and access memory. The model is divided into two main areas: the **stack** and the **heap**.

The Stack

The stack is a region of memory used for short-lived data that is specific to each thread. When a method is called, a stack frame is created to store local variables, method parameters, and other data relevant to that method's execution. Once the method completes, the stack frame is removed, freeing the memory.

- **Characteristics of the Stack**:
    - Memory is automatically allocated and deallocated with method calls.
    - Data in the stack is local to each thread, reducing the risk of concurrent access issues.
    - The stack has limited memory, and deep recursion or excessive method calls can lead to a StackOverflowError.

The Heap

The heap is a larger, more dynamic memory area where objects are allocated. Unlike the stack, memory in the heap is managed by Java's garbage collector (GC), which automatically frees memory when objects are no longer needed. The heap is divided into several regions to optimize memory allocation and garbage collection.

- **Heap Regions**:
    - **Young Generation**: Stores newly created objects, with frequent garbage

collection (Minor GC) to remove short-lived objects.

- **Old Generation**: Holds long-lived objects that survived multiple rounds of garbage collection in the young generation.

- **Metaspace**: Stores metadata for classes, methods, and other structures. Unlike the heap, metaspace is allocated outside the main memory and can grow as needed, though it's still subject to GC.

Garbage Collection (GC)

Garbage collection is the process of identifying and freeing memory occupied by objects that are no longer in use. Java's garbage collector automates this process, reducing the risk of memory leaks. However, understanding how GC works is essential for optimizing memory management in Java applications.

Garbage Collection Mechanisms

Java uses several garbage collection algorithms, each with its own advantages and trade-offs. The choice of algorithm depends on the application's memory requirements, latency tolerance, and throughput needs.

1. **Serial GC**: A simple, single-threaded garbage collector. While efficient for small applications, it may cause performance bottlenecks in larger systems.

2. **Parallel GC (Throughput GC)**: A multi-threaded collector that focuses on maximizing throughput. It performs full GC events in parallel, making it suitable for applications that can tolerate brief pauses in favor of higher overall performance.

3. **CMS (Concurrent Mark-Sweep) GC**: Designed to minimize pause times, the CMS collector works in multiple stages, concurrently sweeping through the heap to free up memory. It's ideal for applications with low-latency requirements, though it can be resource-intensive.

4. **G1 (Garbage-First) GC**: A modern collector introduced in Java 7 and improved in Java 9. G1 GC divides the heap into regions and prioritizes collecting regions with the most garbage, optimizing both latency and throughput.

5. **Z Garbage Collector (ZGC)**: Available in Java 11 and later, ZGC is a low-latency collector capable of handling heaps up to multiple terabytes. It's ideal for applications requiring minimal GC pauses.

How Garbage Collection Works

The garbage collection process typically involves three main phases:

- **Marking**: The GC marks all reachable objects, identifying which ones are still in use.

- **Sweeping**: Unreachable objects (those without references) are marked for removal.

- **Compaction**: The heap is compacted to free up continuous memory blocks, reducing fragmentation.

Understanding the different types of garbage collection can help you select the appropriate strategy for your application. For example, real-time applications with low-latency requirements might benefit from ZGC, while data-intensive applications might prioritize the throughput of G1 GC.

Techniques for Managing Memory Efficiently

Effective memory management involves optimizing both object creation and garbage collection. Here are some strategies for managing memory efficiently in complex applications.

1. Avoiding Unnecessary Object Creation

Creating new objects consumes both CPU and memory resources. Reducing object creation can significantly improve memory efficiency, especially in applications with high object churn.

- **Use Primitives Over Wrapper Classes**: Where possible, use primitive data types (int, double, boolean) instead of wrapper classes (Integer, Double, Boolean). Primitives consume less memory and avoid unnecessary object creation.

- **Reuse Existing Objects**: Use object pooling for frequently used objects. For example, if you need to handle a large number of database connections, a connection pool reuses existing connections rather than creating new ones.

- **Use StringBuilder or StringBuffer for String Manipulation**: Strings in Java are immutable, so each modification creates a new object. Use StringBuilder for mutable string operations to minimize object creation.

2. Leveraging Soft, Weak, and Phantom References

Java provides different types of references (in addition to strong references) to control object lifecycle and garbage collection.

- **Soft References**: Objects with only soft references are retained as long as there's enough memory. Soft references are useful for caching, where you want to keep objects in memory but allow them to be garbage-collected if needed.

- **Weak References**: Objects with weak references are collected during the next GC cycle, making them ideal for objects like listeners that should not prevent garbage collection.

- **Phantom References**: Phantom references allow you to perform actions after an object is garbage-collected. They're rarely used directly but can be useful for resource cleanup.

3. Minimizing Memory Leaks

A memory leak occurs when objects are retained in memory longer than necessary. Memory leaks can cause applications to consume more memory over time, leading to crashes or slow performance.

- **Release Unused Objects**: Nullify references when an object is no longer needed to make it eligible for garbage collection.

- **Avoid Static References to Large Objects**: Static references persist for the lifetime of the class and can lead to memory leaks if used with large or short-lived objects.

- **Use Tools for Leak Detection**: Tools like VisualVM, JProfiler, and Eclipse MAT (Memory Analyzer Tool) can help identify memory leaks by analyzing heap dumps and finding objects with high retention.

4. Profiling and Monitoring Memory Usage

Regularly monitoring memory usage helps detect bottlenecks, leaks, and opportunities for optimization.

- **Use JVM Profilers**: Profilers like VisualVM, JConsole, and YourKit can track memory allocation, garbage collection events, and heap usage.

- **Analyze Heap Dumps**: Taking heap dumps during peak usage can provide insights into memory allocation and identify areas for optimization.

Example: Memory Optimization for Data-Intensive Applications

Let's consider a real-world example of memory optimization for a data-intensive application. Imagine an e-commerce platform that processes large volumes of transaction data and requires efficient memory usage to maintain performance during peak shopping seasons.

Scenario

The e-commerce platform performs tasks such as processing transactions, updating product inventories, and analyzing customer activity. During peak seasons, such as Black Friday or holiday sales, the platform needs to handle millions of transactions within a short time frame. Without proper memory management, the platform may experience performance degradation or even crash due to memory exhaustion.

Solution

1. **Optimize Object Creation and Data Handling**

   o Instead of creating new objects for each transaction, the platform can use object pooling for reusable components like database connections or thread pools.

   o Use primitive data types for processing transaction data to reduce memory consumption. For example, storing product IDs as int rather than Integer can significantly reduce memory usage when dealing with large datasets.

2. **Use Efficient Data Structures**

   o Avoid using ArrayList or HashMap for very large collections of data. Instead, consider using more memory-efficient data structures, such as Trove collections or specialized data structures that minimize memory usage.

- Use ConcurrentHashMap for concurrent access, reducing memory contention when processing large volumes of data across multiple threads.

3. **Implement Caching with Soft References**

   - The platform can use soft references to cache frequently accessed data, such as product information or customer preferences. This cache can be cleared by the GC when memory is low, reducing the risk of OutOfMemoryErrors during peak times.

   - For example, caching product details with soft references allows data to persist in memory when available while allowing garbage collection if memory is needed for higher-priority tasks.

4. **Minimize Memory Leaks**

   - Monitor for memory leaks by checking for objects that retain references unexpectedly. For instance, avoid static references to large collections or temporary data structures that should be discarded after use.

   - Use weak references for listeners or callback objects that should not prevent the garbage collector from freeing memory.

5. Optimize Garbage Collection with G1 GC

- o Configure the JVM to use the G1 GC collector, which is optimized for low-latency, high-throughput applications. G1 GC can be configured to prioritize garbage collection in specific regions, such as the young generation, where short-lived objects are frequent.

- o Fine-tune GC parameters based on profiling data from tools like VisualVM. By adjusting parameters like -XX:MaxGCPauseMillis and -XX:InitiatingHeapOccupancyPercent, you can balance memory usage and GC frequency for optimal performance.

Code Example: Using Soft References for Caching

```java
import java.lang.ref.SoftReference;

import java.util.HashMap;

import java.util.Map;


public class ProductCache {

    private final Map<String, SoftReference<Product>>
productCache = new HashMap<>();
```

```
    public void addProductToCache(String productId,
Product product) {

        productCache.put(productId, new
SoftReference<>(product));

    }


    public Product getProductFromCache(String
productId) {

        SoftReference<Product> ref =
productCache.get(productId);

        return (ref != null) ? ref.get() : null;

    }

}
```

This ProductCache class uses soft references to store product data in memory. When memory is low, the garbage collector will clear the cache automatically, allowing other critical parts of the application to continue functioning.

Conclusion

Efficient memory management is essential for building high-performance Java applications, especially in data-intensive environments. By understanding Java's memory model, optimizing garbage collection, and implementing memory management techniques, you can significantly improve application scalability and stability.

In this chapter, we've covered Java's memory model, garbage collection mechanisms, and best practices for managing memory efficiently. We also explored a practical example of optimizing memory usage in a data-intensive application, demonstrating how careful memory management can improve performance and prevent issues like memory leaks or application crashes. In the following chapters, we'll build on these concepts as we dive deeper into designing and optimizing complex, high-performance Java applications.

Chapter 3: Advanced Java Generics and Functional Programming

Java Generics and functional programming concepts are essential tools for creating versatile, type-safe, and expressive code. Generics help reduce redundancy and catch errors at compile time by enforcing type constraints, while functional programming introduces a declarative style that can streamline complex operations, particularly in data processing and concurrency. With Java 8, functional programming became a powerful part of the language through the introduction of lambda expressions, the Streams API, and a range of other enhancements that make Java code cleaner and more efficient.

In this chapter, we'll dive into advanced use cases for Java generics, explore key functional programming concepts, and demonstrate their application in data processing using Java's Streams API and lambda expressions.

In-Depth Use of Java Generics

Generics allow developers to define classes, interfaces, and methods with type parameters, making them more versatile and type-safe. Java's generics are essential for creating reusable and flexible code structures, particularly when working with collections, data structures, and custom algorithms.

The Basics of Generics

Generics were introduced in Java 5 to allow type parameters in classes and methods. A generic type parameter is specified within angle brackets (<>) and represents a placeholder for a specific data type. For example, List<T> is a generic type where T can represent any object type.

```java
public class Box<T> {

    private T item;


    public void setItem(T item) {

        this.item = item;

    }


    public T getItem() {
```

```
    return item;

  }

}
```

In this example, Box<T> is a generic class that can hold any type T. This flexibility makes the class more reusable while maintaining type safety, as Java will enforce the specified type at compile time.

Advanced Generics Concepts

1. **Bounded Type Parameters**: By using bounded types, we can restrict the types that can be used as parameters. For instance, if we want a type parameter to be restricted to subclasses of Number, we can use extends:

```
public class NumberBox<T extends Number> {

  private T number;


  public double getDoubleValue() {

    return number.doubleValue();

  }

}
```

Here, NumberBox<T> will only accept types that extend Number, such as Integer or Double.

2. **Multiple Type Parameters**: Generics allow for multiple type parameters in a single class or method. This is useful when working with pairs or mappings.

```
public class Pair<K, V> {

    private K key;

    private V value;


    public Pair(K key, V value) {

        this.key = key;

        this.value = value;

    }


    public K getKey() {

        return key;

    }


    public V getValue() {

        return value;

    }

}
```

3. **Wildcards (?)**: Wildcards provide flexibility in handling generics with unknown types. They are commonly used in method arguments to accept any subclass or superclass of a type, depending on the bounds.

   - **Unbounded Wildcards (<?>)**: Accepts any type.

   - **Upper Bounded Wildcards (<? extends T>)**: Accepts T or any subclass of T.

   - **Lower Bounded Wildcards (<? super T>)**: Accepts T or any superclass of T.

```
public void printNumbers(List<? extends Number> numbers) {

  for (Number n : numbers) {

    System.out.println(n);

  }

}
```

In this example, printNumbers accepts any list containing Number or its subclasses, providing flexibility while ensuring type safety.

4. **Generic Methods**: Methods can be defined with their own type parameters, separate from

the class's type parameters. This is useful for
defining flexible utility methods.

```java
public static <T> void printArray(T[] array) {
    for (T element : array) {
        System.out.println(element);
    }
}
```

Here, printArray can print an array of any type.

Common Pitfalls with Generics

While generics are powerful, they come with certain
limitations:

- **Type Erasure**: Java erases generic type
  information at runtime, making it impossible to
  use reflection with generics or create generic
  arrays.

- **Cannot Instantiate Generic Types**:
  Instantiating a generic type with new T() is not
  allowed due to type erasure.

- **Subclassing Issues**: When subclassing a
  generic type, you must handle the type
  parameter properly, as incorrect handling can
  lead to unexpected behavior.

Generics are a crucial tool for creating flexible, reusable code that minimizes runtime errors, making them ideal for collections, data structures, and utility classes.

Leveraging Functional Programming with Java 8+

With Java 8, functional programming became a first-class citizen in Java, enabling a more declarative, concise approach to common programming tasks. Key features of functional programming in Java include lambda expressions, functional interfaces, and the Streams API.

Lambda Expressions

Lambda expressions allow developers to create anonymous functions in a clean and concise way, ideal for scenarios requiring a small function or callback. A lambda expression is defined using the syntax (parameters) -> expression or (parameters) -> { statements }.

java

```
// Traditional anonymous inner class
Runnable r1 = new Runnable() {
```

```java
@Override
public void run() {
    System.out.println("Hello, world!");
}
};
```

```java
// Lambda expression equivalent
Runnable r2 = () -> System.out.println("Hello, world!");
```

Functional Interfaces

A functional interface is an interface with a single abstract method (SAM), which serves as a target for lambda expressions. Java provides several functional interfaces in java.util.function, including:

- **Predicate<T>**: Represents a boolean-valued function, commonly used for filtering.

- **Function<T, R>**: Represents a function that takes an argument and returns a result.

- **Consumer<T>**: Represents an operation that takes a single argument and returns no result.

- **Supplier<T>**: Represents a supplier of results, commonly used for deferred execution.

```
// Example of a Predicate
Predicate<String> isLongString = s -> s.length() > 10;
```

Functional interfaces allow us to define and use functions as first-class citizens, making our code more modular and expressive.

Streams API for Data Processing

The Streams API, introduced in Java 8, is a powerful tool for processing sequences of elements in a functional, declarative style. A stream represents a sequence of elements that can be transformed, filtered, and aggregated using various intermediate and terminal operations.

Creating and Working with Streams

Streams can be created from collections, arrays, or custom sources, and offer a range of operations for manipulating data. Here are some commonly used operations:

1. **Intermediate Operations**:
   - **filter**: Filters elements based on a condition.
   - **map**: Transforms elements into a new form.

- o **sorted**: Sorts elements based on natural order or a comparator.

2. **Terminal Operations**:

- o **collect**: Collects the results into a collection.

- o **forEach**: Iterates over each element.

- o **reduce**: Reduces elements into a single result using an accumulator.

List<String> names = Arrays.asList("Alice", "Bob", "Charlie", "David");

List<String> longNames = names.stream()

  .filter(name -> name.length() > 3)

  .sorted()

  .collect(Collectors.toList());

In this example, a list of names is filtered and sorted, demonstrating how declarative code can replace traditional loops and conditionals for data processing.

Parallel Streams

Java Streams support parallel processing, enabling tasks to be executed concurrently across multiple CPU cores. To create a parallel stream, simply call parallelStream() on a collection or parallel() on an existing stream.

```java
List<Integer> numbers = Arrays.asList(1, 2, 3, 4, 5);
int sum = numbers.parallelStream()
    .mapToInt(Integer::intValue)
    .sum();
```

Parallel streams are particularly useful for computationally intensive tasks but should be used with caution in tasks that involve shared resources or require a predictable order.

Scenario: Data Processing in Parallel with Streams and Lambdas

Let's walk through a scenario that illustrates the power of Java's Streams API and lambda expressions in a data processing task. Imagine we're working with a large dataset of customer orders, and we need to perform several operations on this data, including filtering, mapping, and aggregation.

Problem Statement

Given a list of orders, we need to:

1. Filter out canceled orders.

2. Map each order to the customer's total purchase amount.

3. Calculate the total revenue generated by all completed orders.

4. Perform these operations concurrently to maximize performance.

Solution Using Streams and Parallel Processing

1. **Define the Order Class**: First, we define an Order class to represent each customer order, with properties like status and amount.

```
public class Order {

    private String status;

    private double amount;


    public Order(String status, double amount) {

        this.status = status;

        this.amount = amount;

    }


    public String getStatus() {
```

```java
        return status;

    }


    public double getAmount() {

        return amount;

    }

}
```

2. **Generate a List of Orders**: For demonstration, we generate a list of sample orders.

```java
List<Order> orders = Arrays.asList(

    new Order("completed", 120.0),

    new Order("canceled", 90.0),

    new Order("completed", 200.0),

    new Order("completed", 80.0)

);
```

3. **Process the Orders with Streams**: Using a parallel stream, we filter, map, and aggregate the data in a single pipeline.

```java
double totalRevenue = orders.parallelStream()
```

```
   .filter(order ->
"completed".equals(order.getStatus()))

   .mapToDouble(Order::getAmount)

   .sum();


System.out.println("Total Revenue: $" +
totalRevenue);
```

In this example, we filter orders with a status of completed, map each order to its amount, and sum the results. Using parallelStream() allows this operation to be processed concurrently, improving performance when working with large datasets.

Conclusion

Advanced Java generics and functional programming concepts bring significant power and flexibility to Java development. Generics allow for type-safe, reusable classes and methods, making code more robust and maintainable. Functional programming, with features like lambda expressions and the Streams API, provides a declarative approach to coding, enabling more concise and expressive code.

In this chapter, we covered advanced generics concepts, including bounded types, wildcards, and generic methods. We also explored Java's functional programming features, including lambda expressions, functional interfaces, and the Streams API. Finally, we demonstrated these principles in a practical scenario involving data processing with parallel streams.

Mastering generics and functional programming will empower you to write cleaner, more efficient Java code, especially when handling complex data transformations and parallel processing. As we continue, these principles will serve as a foundation for building high-performance, scalable Java applications.

Chapter 4: Data Structures and Algorithms for High Performance

In high-performance Java applications, choosing the right data structures and algorithms is essential for achieving optimal efficiency and scalability. The selection of a data structure can significantly impact memory usage, processing speed, and overall system performance. This chapter delves into selecting the best data structures for specific application needs, implementing custom structures when necessary, and optimizing algorithms to handle large volumes of data in real-time environments. We'll conclude with a practical example of building a high-speed cache for quick data access.

Optimal Data Structure Choices for Specific Applications

Each data structure has its strengths and weaknesses, and understanding these can help you choose the right one for a given application. Let's go over some key data structures commonly used in high-performance Java applications and discuss scenarios where they excel.

1. ArrayList and LinkedList

- **ArrayList**: Backed by a dynamic array, ArrayList is optimal for applications that require fast access to elements using an index. The downside is that inserting or deleting elements, especially in the middle, can be slow due to array shifting.

  - **Use Case**: Storing a list of items when frequent access is needed, but modifications are minimal, like maintaining a list of search results.

- **LinkedList**: LinkedList is a doubly linked list, which is efficient for inserting and deleting elements at any position. However, random access is slower because it requires traversing the list.

  - **Use Case**: Applications needing frequent insertions and deletions, like a job queue for tasks in a processing pipeline.

2. HashMap and TreeMap

- **HashMap**: Implements a hash table for fast key-value pair storage and retrieval. The average time complexity for operations is $O(1)$, making it ideal for scenarios requiring quick lookups.

- o **Use Case**: A cache or lookup table for mapping user IDs to user details in a web application.

- **TreeMap**: Based on a Red-Black tree, TreeMap maintains a sorted order of keys. However, operations take O(log n) time due to the tree structure.

    - o **Use Case**: Applications that require ordered key-value pairs, such as a leaderboard that displays players sorted by scores.

3. PriorityQueue

- **PriorityQueue**: Implements a binary heap for managing a collection of elements with a priority. It's commonly used for scheduling tasks or selecting the highest/lowest priority elements.

    - o **Use Case**: Task scheduling in real-time applications where the next task is determined by priority, such as a scheduler for managing system resources.

4. Concurrent Data Structures

In multi-threaded applications, concurrent data structures help maintain performance and avoid thread-safety issues. Java's java.util.concurrent package provides several of these, including:

- **ConcurrentHashMap**: A thread-safe hash table optimized for concurrent read and write operations.

  - **Use Case**: A shared in-memory cache in a web application accessed by multiple threads.

- **CopyOnWriteArrayList**: Optimized for read-heavy workloads with minimal modifications. When a write occurs, the list is copied to maintain thread safety.

  - **Use Case**: A frequently-read configuration list in a high-availability system that changes infrequently.

5. ArrayDeque and Stack

- **ArrayDeque**: A double-ended queue implemented using an array, providing fast insertions and deletions at both ends.

  - **Use Case**: As a stack or a queue in real-time applications, like a backtracking algorithm for pathfinding.

- **Stack**: While Java includes a Stack class, ArrayDeque is generally faster and more versatile for stack operations.

o **Use Case**: Recursion and undo functionality, like an editor with an undo stack.

Implementing Custom Data Structures

Sometimes, built-in data structures may not fully meet the needs of an application, particularly when high performance and specific requirements are involved. Implementing custom data structures can help optimize memory usage, improve access speeds, or create specialized structures for unique use cases.

Custom Hash Table with Specialized Collision Resolution

A hash table provides efficient key-value storage, but high collision rates can degrade performance. Java's HashMap uses linked lists for collision resolution, but an application may benefit from alternative strategies like open addressing, where collisions are resolved by probing alternative slots.

java

```java
public class CustomHashTable<K, V> {
    private Object[] table;
```

```java
    private int size;

    public CustomHashTable(int capacity) {
        table = new Object[capacity];
        size = 0;
    }

    public void put(K key, V value) {
        int index = hash(key);
        while (table[index] != null) {
            index = (index + 1) % table.length; // Linear probing
        }
        table[index] = new Entry<>(key, value);
        size++;
    }

    public V get(K key) {
        int index = hash(key);
        while (table[index] != null) {
```

```java
        Entry<K, V> entry = (Entry<K, V>)
table[index];

        if (entry.key.equals(key)) return entry.value;

        index = (index + 1) % table.length;

    }

    return null;

}


private int hash(K key) {
    return Math.abs(key.hashCode()) % table.length;
}


private static class Entry<K, V> {
    K key;
    V value;

    Entry(K key, V value) {
        this.key = key;
        this.value = value;
    }
}
```

}

In this CustomHashTable example, we use open addressing with linear probing to resolve collisions. This approach minimizes memory usage by avoiding linked lists, making it suitable for high-performance applications with predictable access patterns.

Custom Linked List for Real-Time Processing

Linked lists are typically implemented with a head and tail, but specific applications might require circular or doubly linked structures with specialized features. For instance, a circular buffer can be created using a custom linked list, which is efficient for real-time applications needing a fixed-size queue.

Algorithm Optimizations

The efficiency of data processing tasks depends heavily on the algorithms chosen. Optimizing algorithms can make a significant difference in execution time, especially when dealing with large datasets.

Sorting Algorithms

- **QuickSort**: Performs well on average, with O(n log n) complexity, making it suitable for general-purpose sorting.

- **MergeSort**: Stable and efficient, especially for large datasets that require sorting external memory.

- **RadixSort**: Ideal for sorting integers or strings with a fixed range, offering O(n) complexity.

Search Algorithms

- **Binary Search**: Efficient for sorted data structures, offering O(log n) time complexity.

- **Hash-Based Lookup**: O(1) average complexity for search, making hash tables like HashMap ideal for quick lookups.

Graph Algorithms for Connectivity

Graph algorithms are vital in applications involving connectivity, like pathfinding or network analysis. Optimizing these algorithms can greatly improve performance in complex systems.

- **Dijkstra's Algorithm**: Finds the shortest path in weighted graphs.

- *A Search**: Combines heuristic optimization with Dijkstra's algorithm for faster pathfinding in real-time applications.

Example: Creating a High-Speed Cache for Real-Time Data Access

Let's build a high-performance cache to demonstrate the selection and customization of data structures. This cache will be optimized for real-time data access, providing a fixed size to prevent memory overflow, and a Least Recently Used (LRU) eviction policy to discard unused items.

Problem Statement

A web application requires a high-speed cache to store user sessions and preferences. To maintain optimal performance, the cache should:

1. Quickly retrieve session data for logged-in users.

2. Evict the least recently used sessions when the cache reaches maximum capacity.

Solution Using LRU Cache

An LRU cache can be implemented using a combination of HashMap and Doubly LinkedList. The HashMap provides O(1) lookup and insertion, while the doubly linked list maintains the order of usage, enabling quick eviction of the least recently used item.

1. **Define the LRU Cache Class**:

```java
import java.util.HashMap;

public class LRUCache<K, V> {
    private final int capacity;
    private HashMap<K, Node<K, V>> cache;
    private Node<K, V> head, tail;

    public LRUCache(int capacity) {
        this.capacity = capacity;
        this.cache = new HashMap<>();
    }

    // Method to get value from cache
    public V get(K key) {
        if (!cache.containsKey(key)) return null;
```

```java
        Node<K, V> node = cache.get(key);
        moveToHead(node);
        return node.value;
    }


    // Method to put value into cache
    public void put(K key, V value) {
        if (cache.containsKey(key)) {
            Node<K, V> node = cache.get(key);
            node.value = value;
            moveToHead(node);
        } else {
            Node<K, V> newNode = new Node<>(key,
value);
            if (cache.size() == capacity) {
                removeTail();
            }
            cache.put(key, newNode);
            addNode(newNode);
        }
    }
```

```java
private void addNode(Node<K, V> node) {
    node.next = head;
    node.prev = null;
    if (head != null) head.prev = node;
    head = node;
    if (tail == null) tail = node;
}

private void moveToHead(Node<K, V> node) {
    if (node == head) return;
    if (node == tail) tail = tail.prev;
    removeNode(node);
    addNode(node);
}

private void removeNode(Node<K, V> node) {
    if (node.prev != null) node.prev.next = node.next;
    if (node.next != null) node.next.prev = node.prev;
}
```

```java
private void removeTail() {
    if (tail != null) {
        cache.remove(tail.key);
        tail = tail.prev;
        if (tail != null) tail.next = null;
    }
}

private static class Node<K, V> {
    K key;
    V value;
    Node<K, V> prev, next;

    Node(K key, V value) {
        this.key = key;
        this.value = value;
    }
}
}
```

2. **Using the LRU Cache**

```java
public class Main {

    public static void main(String[] args) {

        LRUCache<String, String> sessionCache = new
LRUCache<>(3);

        sessionCache.put("user1", "session1");

        sessionCache.put("user2", "session2");

        sessionCache.put("user3", "session3");


        System.out.println(sessionCache.get("user1")); //
Accesses user1's session

        sessionCache.put("user4", "session4"); // Evicts
user2's session (LRU)

        System.out.println(sessionCache.get("user2")); //
Returns null (evicted)

    }

}
```

In this implementation:

- When a key is accessed or added, it's moved to the head of the doubly linked list.

- When the cache reaches capacity, the tail (least recently used) node is evicted.

Conclusion

Choosing the right data structures and algorithms is crucial for high-performance Java applications. Understanding the strengths of various data structures, customizing them for specific needs, and optimizing algorithms for fast execution can significantly enhance application efficiency. In this chapter, we covered optimal data structure choices, custom implementations, and a practical example of building an LRU cache for real-time data access. These principles form the foundation for efficient Java programming, enabling you to build responsive, scalable applications.

Chapter 5: Advanced Exception Handling and Logging

Error handling and logging are critical components of building robust, scalable applications. They allow developers to anticipate potential issues, capture detailed information for diagnostics, and ensure system resilience even in the face of unexpected errors. In this chapter, we explore advanced exception handling strategies for enterprise applications, best practices for logging and monitoring application health, and demonstrate practical implementation in a microservices architecture.

Robust Error Handling Strategies for Enterprise Applications

In an enterprise environment, applications handle complex operations, often involving various interconnected services, APIs, and databases. Effective error handling becomes crucial for providing a seamless user experience and maintaining system reliability. Here are strategies for implementing robust error handling in Java.

1. Centralizing Error Handling

Centralized error handling simplifies maintenance by capturing and handling exceptions in one location. In web applications, this can be achieved using a global exception handler.

- **Controller Advice in Spring Boot**: In Spring Boot applications, the @ControllerAdvice annotation allows centralized exception handling for all controllers, reducing repetitive error-handling code across controllers.

```
@ControllerAdvice

public class GlobalExceptionHandler {


@ExceptionHandler(ResourceNotFoundException.class)

    public ResponseEntity<String>
handleResourceNotFound(ResourceNotFoundException ex) {

        return new ResponseEntity<>(ex.getMessage(),
HttpStatus.NOT_FOUND);

    }


    @ExceptionHandler(Exception.class)
```

```java
    public ResponseEntity<String>
handleGeneralException(Exception ex) {

        return new ResponseEntity<>("An error occurred:
" + ex.getMessage(),
HttpStatus.INTERNAL_SERVER_ERROR);

    }

}
```

In this example, specific exceptions are handled (e.g., ResourceNotFoundException) and a generic exception handler for any other errors. This approach ensures consistent error responses across the application.

2. Using Custom Exceptions

Custom exceptions provide clarity and detail about specific error conditions, making debugging easier and improving code readability. Define custom exceptions for distinct error scenarios in your application, and handle them appropriately.

- **Creating Custom Exceptions**:

```java
public class InvalidOrderException extends
RuntimeException {

    public InvalidOrderException(String message) {

        super(message);

    }
```

}

Custom exceptions like InvalidOrderException make it clear what kind of error has occurred and can be used for detailed logging or specific handling.

3. Wrapping and Propagating Exceptions

Exception wrapping is useful when one module calls another and you need to capture the original exception context. By wrapping exceptions, you can retain the stack trace and details while adding additional context.

- **Example of Wrapping Exceptions**:

```
public void processOrder(Order order) {
    try {
        orderService.process(order);
    } catch (SQLException ex) {
        throw new OrderProcessingException("Failed to process order", ex);
    }
}
```

In this example, the SQLException is wrapped in a custom OrderProcessingException, preserving the root cause while providing more context for debugging.

4. Using Finally and Try-With-Resources for Resource Management

When dealing with resources like files, streams, or database connections, it's essential to release them properly. Java's try-with-resources statement automatically closes resources, helping to prevent memory leaks.

```java
try (FileInputStream fis = new FileInputStream("data.txt")) {

    // Read from file

} catch (IOException ex) {

    // Handle exception

}
```

In this case, FileInputStream is automatically closed, even if an exception occurs, simplifying resource management.

5. Graceful Degradation

Graceful degradation is an approach where, in case of an error, the application continues to provide essential functions. This can improve the user experience by allowing the application to remain partially functional.

For instance, if a non-critical service fails, you might show cached data instead of an error message, or notify users of limited functionality rather than stopping the application.

Best Practices for Logging and Monitoring Application Health

Logging and monitoring provide insight into an application's behavior, helping developers to track errors, performance, and usage patterns. Effective logging and monitoring are vital in large-scale systems to identify issues proactively and maintain a high level of reliability.

1. Structuring and Categorizing Logs

Categorize logs into different levels to structure the output and ensure relevant information is captured without overwhelming the logs.

- **Log Levels**:
    - **INFO**: General information about application flow, such as successful startup or shutdown messages.
    - **DEBUG**: Detailed information for debugging, generally disabled in production due to verbosity.
    - **WARN**: Indications of potential issues, such as deprecated API usage or unexpected but non-critical conditions.

- **ERROR**: Significant issues that affect normal operation, such as failed database connections or failed external API calls.

- **FATAL**: Severe errors that cause application shutdown or critical failures.

```
private static final Logger logger =
LoggerFactory.getLogger(MyClass.class);


public void processOrder(Order order) {

    logger.info("Processing order with ID: {}",
order.getId());

    try {

        // Process order

    } catch (Exception ex) {

        logger.error("Error processing order with ID: {}",
order.getId(), ex);

    }

}
```

2. Adding Context to Logs

Contextual information, such as user ID, session ID, or order ID, is invaluable for tracking specific operations across the application and identifying root causes in complex scenarios.

- **Example of Adding Context**:

```java
public void checkoutOrder(Order order) {

    logger.info("Initiating checkout for order ID: {}", order.getId());

    try {

        paymentService.processPayment(order);

    } catch (PaymentException ex) {

        logger.error("Payment failed for order ID: {}", order.getId(), ex);

    }

}
```

3. Using External Log Aggregation Tools

For enterprise applications, external log aggregation tools provide powerful search, filtering, and alerting capabilities, simplifying log analysis and monitoring. Popular tools include:

- **ELK Stack** (Elasticsearch, Logstash, and Kibana): Provides real-time search and visualization of logs.

- **Splunk**: An enterprise-level tool for monitoring, searching, and analyzing log data.

- **Graylog**: A centralized logging solution that aggregates and visualizes log data.

4. Implementing Monitoring and Health Checks

Monitoring tools provide insights into the health of your application and help track performance metrics like CPU usage, memory consumption, and request latency. Health checks ensure that services are operational, alerting administrators when failures occur.

- **Prometheus** and **Grafana**: Prometheus is a monitoring tool that collects metrics from applications, while Grafana provides visualization and dashboarding capabilities.

- **Spring Boot Actuator**: For Spring Boot applications, Actuator exposes health check endpoints that provide information about application health, memory usage, and other metrics.

Example of a Health Check Endpoint Using Spring Boot Actuator:

yaml

```yaml
management:
  endpoints:
    web:
      exposure:
```

include: "health"

This configuration enables a /actuator/health endpoint, which can be integrated with monitoring tools for real-time health tracking.

Practical Case: Logging and Error Handling in a Microservices Setup

In microservices architectures, each service operates independently, communicating with other services over the network. Implementing consistent logging and error-handling practices across services is essential for diagnosing issues and maintaining reliability. Here, we'll look at a practical scenario of handling errors and logging in a microservices environment for an e-commerce platform.

Scenario Overview

An e-commerce platform has multiple microservices:

1. **Order Service**: Handles customer orders.

2. **Inventory Service**: Manages product inventory.

3. **Payment Service**: Processes payments.

Each service communicates with others over REST APIs, and each has its own database and logging setup.

Step-by-Step Implementation

Step 1: Centralized Logging Across Microservices

Use a centralized logging approach to collect logs from each microservice in a single location. This allows developers to trace operations that span multiple services and identify issues across the system.

- **Using ELK Stack for Log Aggregation**: Install and configure Elasticsearch, Logstash, and Kibana. Configure each microservice to send logs to a centralized location using a logging library compatible with Logstash, such as **Logback** with JSON format.

Logback Configuration Example:

xml

```xml
<configuration>
    <appender name="LOGSTASH" class="net.logstash.logback.appender.LogstashTcpSocketAppender">
        <destination>logstash-host:5000</destination>
    </appender>
    <root level="INFO">
        <appender-ref ref="LOGSTASH" />
    </root>
</configuration>
```

This configuration sends logs from the microservices to Logstash, which forwards them to Elasticsearch for centralized storage and makes them searchable in Kibana.

Step 2: Implementing Contextual Logging in Microservices

Pass a unique trace ID through each service call to track an individual request across multiple services. This ID allows you to trace the lifecycle of a request as it moves between services.

- **Propagating Trace IDs**: Generate a trace ID at the start of a request (e.g., in the Order Service) and include it in HTTP headers when calling other services (e.g., Inventory Service and Payment Service). Each service logs the trace ID, providing a way to correlate logs.

```
public ResponseEntity<?> placeOrder(Order order) {

    String traceId = UUID.randomUUID().toString();

    MDC.put("traceId", traceId);

    logger.info("Placing order with trace ID: {}", traceId);


    // Call to Inventory Service and Payment Service with traceId
```

```
// ...
```

```
MDC.clear(); // Clear context after request is processed
}
```

Step 3: Error Handling and Fallbacks

Implement fallback mechanisms to ensure the application degrades gracefully in case of service failures. For instance, if the Payment Service fails, the Order Service should roll back the transaction or notify the user of the issue.

- **Using Circuit Breaker Pattern with Resilience4j**: Resilience4j is a library that provides fault-tolerant patterns like circuit breakers. Circuit breakers prevent cascading failures by halting calls to a failed service until it's healthy again.

Example of Circuit Breaker in Order Service:

```
@Service
public class OrderService {

    private final PaymentService paymentService;
```

```java
    public OrderService(PaymentService
paymentService) {

        this.paymentService = paymentService;

    }


    @CircuitBreaker(name = "paymentService",
fallbackMethod = "fallbackPayment")

    public void processPayment(Order order) {

        paymentService.pay(order);

    }


    public void fallbackPayment(Order order,
Throwable ex) {

        logger.error("Payment failed for order ID: {}.
Falling back.", order.getId(), ex);

        // Handle fallback, e.g., notify user or retry later

    }
}
```

When the Payment Service fails, the fallbackPayment method is triggered, logging the error and handling it gracefully by notifying the user or implementing a retry mechanism.

Step 4: Health Checks and Monitoring

Enable health checks and monitoring across services to monitor application health proactively.

- **Using Spring Boot Actuator for Health Checks**: Enable health endpoints on each microservice using Spring Boot Actuator, allowing tools like Prometheus to monitor each service's health.

yaml

```yaml
management:
  endpoints:
    web:
      exposure:
        include: "health,metrics"
```

This configuration exposes the /actuator/health and /actuator/metrics endpoints, providing visibility into each service's health and resource usage.

Conclusion

In this chapter, we explored advanced exception handling and logging practices that are essential for building resilient and maintainable Java applications. Effective error handling and logging are especially important in enterprise environments, where application stability and diagnostics are critical.

Implementing robust error handling strategies, including centralized exception handling, custom exceptions, and graceful degradation, enables Java applications to recover from errors and continue operating smoothly. With structured logging, contextual information, and centralized log aggregation, developers can monitor application health and troubleshoot issues effectively. In a microservices architecture, consistent logging, tracing, and monitoring practices allow developers to manage complex distributed systems reliably.

By applying these techniques, Java developers can build scalable, high-performance applications that deliver a seamless user experience and are resilient in the face of unexpected challenges.

Part 2
Building Scalable Systems in Java

Chapter 6: Distributed Computing Fundamentals

Distributed computing is the foundation of many modern applications, enabling systems to divide tasks among multiple machines or services. With the rise of cloud computing, microservices, and data-intensive applications, understanding distributed systems has become essential for Java developers building scalable, high-performance applications. This chapter explores the fundamentals of distributed systems, Java's support for distributed computing with tools like RMI and gRPC, the challenges inherent in distributed architectures, and strategies for overcoming these challenges. We'll conclude with a practical case study on building a load-balanced storage system.

Basics of Distributed Systems

A distributed system is a collection of independent computers that work together to perform a unified task. Each component, or node, in a distributed system can run independently, but they communicate with one another to share data, process tasks, and deliver results.

Key Components of Distributed Systems

1. **Nodes**: Independent computers or services that make up the distributed system. Each node runs its own instances of software and communicates with other nodes.

2. **Communication Protocol**: The method by which nodes communicate and share data. In Java, common protocols include Remote Method Invocation (RMI), HTTP, and gRPC.

3. **Data Sharing and Consistency**: Data must be shared between nodes, either through a centralized database, replicated data stores, or messaging systems.

4. **Fault Tolerance**: The ability of the system to continue functioning even if one or more nodes fail.

5. **Scalability**: Distributed systems are designed to handle increased load by adding more nodes,

making them suitable for high-demand applications.

Examples of Distributed Systems

- **Microservices**: An architecture in which applications are broken into smaller, independent services, each running on separate nodes.

- **Cluster Computing**: A collection of nodes working on tasks collectively, commonly used in high-performance computing.

- **Distributed Databases**: Databases that store data across multiple nodes to improve availability and scalability, such as Apache Cassandra or Google's Bigtable.

Distributed systems have become essential for scaling applications in cloud environments, handling large volumes of data, and providing high availability.

Java Support for Distributed Computing

Java provides several tools and frameworks that simplify the process of building distributed applications. Two popular options are **Remote Method Invocation (RMI)** and **gRPC**.

1. Remote Method Invocation (RMI)

RMI allows Java objects to communicate over a network by invoking methods on remote objects as if they were local. It uses Java's built-in serialization to pass objects and method parameters between the client and server.

- **Advantages**:
    - Simplifies the development of Java-only distributed applications.
    - Provides a synchronous and type-safe communication mechanism.

- **Disadvantages**:
    - Limited to Java applications, making it less suitable for polyglot environments.
    - Less efficient than modern alternatives like gRPC due to its reliance on Java serialization.

Example of RMI in Java:

```
// Define a remote interface
import java.rmi.Remote;
```

```java
import java.rmi.RemoteException;

public interface HelloService extends Remote {
    String sayHello(String name) throws
RemoteException;
}


// Implement the remote interface
import java.rmi.server.UnicastRemoteObject;

public class HelloServiceImpl extends
UnicastRemoteObject implements HelloService {
    public HelloServiceImpl() throws RemoteException
{ super(); }

    public String sayHello(String name) throws
RemoteException {
        return "Hello, " + name;
    }
}

// Server code
```

```java
import java.rmi.registry.LocateRegistry;
import java.rmi.registry.Registry;

public class RmiServer {
    public static void main(String[] args) {
        try {
            HelloService helloService = new HelloServiceImpl();
            Registry registry = LocateRegistry.createRegistry(1099);
            registry.bind("HelloService", helloService);
            System.out.println("RMI Server started.");
        } catch (Exception e) {
            e.printStackTrace();
        }
    }
}

// Client code
import java.rmi.registry.LocateRegistry;
import java.rmi.registry.Registry;
```

```java
public class RmiClient {

    public static void main(String[] args) {

        try {

            Registry registry =
LocateRegistry.getRegistry("localhost", 1099);

            HelloService helloService = (HelloService)
registry.lookup("HelloService");

            System.out.println(helloService.sayHello("Java
Developer"));

        } catch (Exception e) {

            e.printStackTrace();

        }

    }

}
```

2. gRPC (gRPC Remote Procedure Call)

gRPC is an open-source RPC framework developed by Google that enables efficient, language-independent communication between services. It uses Protocol Buffers (protobuf) for serialization, which is faster and more compact than Java's built-in serialization.

- **Advantages**:

- Supports multiple languages, making it suitable for polyglot environments.

- Offers efficient binary serialization with Protocol Buffers.

- Built-in support for bidirectional streaming, enabling asynchronous communication.

- **Disadvantages**:

  - Requires learning Protocol Buffers and setting up the gRPC framework.

  - Can be more complex to configure and manage than simpler HTTP-based communication.

Example of gRPC in Java (simplified):

1. Define the gRPC service in a .proto file.

proto

```
syntax = "proto3";


service HelloService {
  rpc sayHello (HelloRequest) returns (HelloResponse);
}
```

```
message HelloRequest {

    string name = 1;

}


message HelloResponse {

    string message = 1;

}
```

2. Compile the .proto file with the gRPC compiler to generate Java code.
3. Implement the generated gRPC service in Java.

```java
import io.grpc.stub.StreamObserver;


public class HelloServiceImpl extends
HelloServiceGrpc.HelloServiceImplBase {

    @Override

    public void sayHello(HelloRequest request,
StreamObserver<HelloResponse> responseObserver)
{

        String message = "Hello, " + request.getName();
```

```
    HelloResponse response =
HelloResponse.newBuilder().setMessage(message).bui
ld();

    responseObserver.onNext(response);

    responseObserver.onCompleted();

  }

}
```

4. Configure and run the gRPC server and client.

gRPC is widely used for inter-service communication in microservices, data streaming applications, and IoT, thanks to its efficiency and compatibility with multiple languages.

Challenges and Strategies for Building Distributed Java Applications

While distributed systems offer significant benefits, they come with challenges that require careful planning and design. Let's examine some common challenges and strategies to address them.

1. Network Reliability

Distributed applications rely on network communication, which can introduce latency, data loss, and temporary disconnections.

- **Strategy**: Implement retries, timeouts, and circuit breakers to handle network failures gracefully. Frameworks like Netflix Hystrix provide circuit breaker implementations to detect and manage failed requests.

2. Data Consistency

Maintaining consistency across distributed nodes is challenging, especially in applications that require real-time data updates.

- **Strategy**: Use consistency models based on the application's needs:

  - **Strong Consistency**: Guarantees all nodes have the same data, but can be slower. Use for critical data like financial transactions.

  - **Eventual Consistency**: Allows for temporary inconsistencies, with data eventually syncing. Suitable for non-critical data like social media feeds.

3. Fault Tolerance and Resilience

Distributed systems must handle node failures gracefully without impacting the overall system.

- **Strategy**: Use redundancy and replication to ensure high availability. Design components to be stateless or use persistent storage to enable fast recovery.

4. Distributed Transactions

Handling transactions across distributed services can be complex, as a single failure could leave data in an inconsistent state.

- **Strategy**: Use the Two-Phase Commit (2PC) protocol for critical transactions or the SAGA pattern, which breaks down a transaction into a series of steps with compensating actions in case of failure.

5. Scalability and Load Balancing

Scaling a distributed application can be challenging, particularly when workloads vary significantly.

- **Strategy**: Implement load balancing to distribute workloads across nodes evenly. Load balancers can use strategies such as round-robin or least connections to determine the best node for handling a request.

Case Study: A Load-Balanced Storage System

Let's walk through a practical example of building a load-balanced, distributed storage system for a hypothetical company that stores and processes large volumes of data in real-time.

Problem Statement

The company needs a storage system that can:

1. Handle millions of data requests daily.

2. Distribute data storage across multiple nodes to avoid overloading any single node.

3. Ensure data availability and fault tolerance, so data remains accessible even if one node fails.

Solution Design

1. System Architecture

The storage system will have multiple storage nodes that store data independently. A load balancer will direct incoming requests to the appropriate storage node based on the current load. Each node has a replica for fault tolerance, so data is never lost if one node fails.

2. Choosing the Right Tools

- gRPC: Used for communication between the load balancer and storage nodes due to its high efficiency and support for bidirectional streaming.

- **Consistent Hashing**: A load-balancing strategy that maps data to storage nodes based on a hash function, minimizing data movement when new nodes are added or removed.

- **Replicated Storage**: Each node has a replica, ensuring data redundancy and fault tolerance.

3. **Implementing Load Balancing with Consistent Hashing**

Consistent hashing maps data requests to storage nodes, minimizing disruptions when nodes are added or removed.

```
public class ConsistentHashing {

    private TreeMap<Integer, String> nodeMap = new
    TreeMap<>();

    private static final int REPLICA_FACTOR = 3;


    public void addNode(String nodeId) {

        for (int i = 0; i < REPLICA_FACTOR; i++) {
```

```java
        int hash = hashFunction(nodeId + i);

        nodeMap.put(hash, nodeId);

    }

}


public String getNode(String dataKey) {

    int hash = hashFunction(dataKey);

    if (!nodeMap.containsKey(hash)) {

        return
nodeMap.get(nodeMap.ceilingKey(hash));

    }

    return nodeMap.get(hash);

}


private int hashFunction(String key) {

    return key.hashCode() % 1000;

}

}
```

4. **Handling Failures with Replica Nodes**

When a storage node fails, requests are redirected to the node's replica to ensure availability.

java

```java
public String getReplicaNode(String nodeId) {
    return replicaMap.get(nodeId);
}
```

Conclusion

Distributed computing is essential for building scalable, high-performance applications that handle large amounts of data. This chapter covered the basics of distributed systems, Java's support for distributed applications with RMI and gRPC, and strategies for overcoming distributed computing challenges. Through a case study on a load-balanced storage system, we illustrated how to design a resilient distributed application using Java.

Understanding these fundamentals will empower you to build applications that scale efficiently, handle failures gracefully, and maintain data consistency across nodes.

Chapter 7: Microservices Architecture with Java

Microservices architecture has transformed how applications are developed and deployed, especially in large-scale enterprise environments. By breaking down applications into smaller, independently deployable services, microservices enable rapid scaling, improved fault tolerance, and easier maintenance. In this chapter, we'll explore the core principles of microservices, discuss how to use Java's Spring Boot framework for microservice design, and address critical challenges in inter-service communication and data consistency. We'll conclude with a practical example of building a scalable user authentication microservice.

Core Principles of Microservices Architecture

Microservices architecture involves dividing an application into smaller, loosely coupled services, each responsible for a specific piece of functionality. Each microservice can be developed, deployed, and scaled independently, which makes this approach well-suited for applications that need to handle high traffic and require rapid updates.

1. Characteristics of Microservices

- **Independently Deployable Services**: Each microservice is an independent component that can be developed, deployed, and scaled independently of the others.

- **Single Responsibility Principle**: Each service should focus on a specific function or business capability, such as user management, payment processing, or order handling.

- **Decentralized Data Management**: Each microservice manages its own data, often using its own database. This approach reduces data coupling and minimizes dependencies between services.

- **Resilience and Fault Tolerance**: Microservices should be designed to handle failures gracefully. When a service fails, it shouldn't bring down the entire application.

- **Continuous Delivery and Deployment**: Microservices support rapid development and deployment cycles, enabling teams to release new features and fixes quickly.

2. Benefits of Microservices Architecture

- **Scalability**: Microservices can be scaled independently, allowing high-demand services to scale without impacting others.

- **Agility**: Teams can work on different services simultaneously, reducing development time and enabling faster delivery.

- **Fault Isolation**: Failures in one service are isolated from others, improving application resilience.

- **Technology Diversity**: Each microservice can use different technologies, frameworks, or databases based on its requirements.

3. Challenges of Microservices Architecture

While microservices offer many advantages, they introduce certain challenges that need to be managed carefully:

- **Complexity**: Managing multiple services increases overall system complexity, especially in deployment, monitoring, and inter-service communication.

- **Data Consistency**: Each service has its own data, which can lead to consistency issues across services, particularly in transactions.

- **Service Discovery and Load Balancing**: Identifying and routing requests to the appropriate instances of a service requires service discovery and load-balancing mechanisms.

- **Inter-Service Communication**: Services need to communicate effectively, which involves choosing the right communication protocols and handling errors gracefully.

Using Spring Boot for Microservice Design

Spring Boot is a popular framework for building Java-based microservices due to its ease of setup, powerful configuration options, and extensive ecosystem. Spring

Boot simplifies dependency management, configuration, and application setup, allowing developers to focus on core functionality.

1. Setting Up a Microservice with Spring Boot

Spring Boot provides a fast and efficient way to create REST APIs, which are commonly used to expose microservices. Here's a quick guide to setting up a simple microservice with Spring Boot.

1. **Create a New Spring Boot Project**: Use Spring Initializr (https://start.spring.io/) or your IDE to create a new Spring Boot project with dependencies like Spring Web, Spring Data JPA, and MySQL Driver (or any other database driver).

2. **Define the Service Layer**: Each microservice is designed to perform a specific function. For example, a user service could manage user accounts, registration, and profiles.

3. **Expose RESTful Endpoints**: Use Spring's @RestController to define endpoints for handling HTTP requests, making it easy to interact with the service.

4. **Use Spring Data JPA for Data Access**: Spring Data JPA simplifies database access by abstracting common operations such as CRUD, freeing developers from writing repetitive SQL code.

Example:

```java
@RestController
@RequestMapping("/users")
public class UserController {

    @Autowired
    private UserService userService;

    @PostMapping("/register")
    public ResponseEntity<User>
    registerUser(@RequestBody User user) {
        User registeredUser = userService.register(user);
        return new ResponseEntity<>(registeredUser,
    HttpStatus.CREATED);
    }

    @GetMapping("/{id}")
    public ResponseEntity<User>
    getUserById(@PathVariable Long id) {
        User user = userService.getUserById(id);
```

```
    return new ResponseEntity<>(user,
HttpStatus.OK);

    }

}
```

2. Configuring Each Microservice Independently

Each microservice is a standalone application, and
Spring Boot provides the necessary tools to configure
them independently:

- **Application Configuration**: Each service has
  its own application.properties or
  application.yml file, where you can define
  specific properties such as server ports,
  database connections, and service-specific
  configurations.

- **Environment Profiles**: Spring Boot supports
  profiles (e.g., dev, test, prod), which allow you
  to configure different settings for different
  environments.

3. Spring Cloud for Microservices

Spring Cloud extends Spring Boot, providing tools and
libraries that make microservices easier to manage.
Some key Spring Cloud components include:

- **Spring Cloud Netflix**: Provides integration
  with Netflix's tools, such as Eureka for service
  discovery and Ribbon for load balancing.

- **Spring Cloud Config**: Allows centralized configuration for all services, enabling easy management of configuration files.

- **Spring Cloud Gateway**: Acts as an API gateway, handling routing, load balancing, and security for requests to microservices.

Managing Inter-Service Communication and Data Consistency

In microservices, inter-service communication and data consistency are crucial for building a cohesive system. Java offers several tools and frameworks for managing these aspects in distributed applications.

1. Inter-Service Communication

Microservices often need to interact with one another. There are two main approaches to inter-service communication:

- **Synchronous Communication (HTTP/REST, gRPC)**: Services communicate in real-time, typically using REST APIs or gRPC. This approach is straightforward but can lead to tight coupling and cascading failures if a service is unavailable.

- o **Spring WebClient**: A non-blocking, reactive client for making HTTP calls between services.

- o **Feign**: A declarative HTTP client that simplifies REST client creation and integrates well with Spring Cloud.

- **Asynchronous Communication (Message Brokers)**: Services communicate by sending messages to a message broker (e.g., Kafka, RabbitMQ), which distributes them to other services. Asynchronous communication is more resilient but adds complexity.

- o **Spring Cloud Stream**: A framework for connecting microservices to message brokers, enabling event-driven communication.

- o **RabbitMQ or Kafka**: Commonly used for asynchronous message passing, reducing dependencies between services.

2. Ensuring Data Consistency Across Services

Maintaining data consistency is one of the main challenges in microservices. Since each service has its own database, ensuring consistent updates across multiple services requires careful design.

- **Event-Driven Architecture**: Services emit events when data changes. Other services subscribe to these events and update their own data accordingly. This approach provides eventual consistency, where data may not be immediately consistent but will converge over time.

- **SAGA Pattern**: For distributed transactions, the SAGA pattern breaks down a transaction into smaller steps with compensating actions for failure scenarios. Each service completes its part of the transaction independently, and compensating actions are used to roll back in case of failure.

Example: Scalable User Authentication Microservice

Let's build a simple, scalable user authentication microservice as an example of using microservices architecture in Java. This service will handle user authentication and generate JWT (JSON Web Tokens) for access control.

Problem Statement

In a large-scale application, users need to authenticate securely, and other services need to verify user identities. The authentication service should:

1. Validate user credentials.
2. Generate a JWT for authenticated users.
3. Integrate with other microservices to authorize access.

Solution Using Spring Boot and JWT

1. **Define the Authentication Service**

   o The service will expose an endpoint (/auth/login) for logging in and an endpoint (/auth/validate) for validating JWTs.

Controller:

```
@RestController
@RequestMapping("/auth")
public class AuthController {

    @Autowired
    private AuthService authService;
```

```java
@PostMapping("/login")

public ResponseEntity<String>
login(@RequestBody LoginRequest loginRequest) {

    String token =
authService.authenticateUser(loginRequest);

    return ResponseEntity.ok(token);

}


@GetMapping("/validate")

public ResponseEntity<Boolean>
validateToken(@RequestParam String token) {

    boolean isValid =
authService.validateToken(token);

    return ResponseEntity.ok(isValid);

}

}
```

2. Implement JWT Authentication

JWT provides a secure way to verify user identities.
When a user logs in, the service will issue a JWT that
can be validated by other services.

- **Generating JWT**:

```java
public String generateToken(String username) {
```

```java
    return Jwts.builder()

        .setSubject(username)

        .setIssuedAt(new Date())

        .setExpiration(new
Date(System.currentTimeMillis() +
TOKEN_EXPIRY))

        .signWith(SignatureAlgorithm.HS256,
SECRET_KEY)

        .compact();
}
```

- o **Validating JWT**:

```java
public boolean validateToken(String token) {
    try {

Jwts.parser().setSigningKey(SECRET_KEY).parseCla
imsJws(token);
        return true;
    } catch (JwtException e) {
        return false;
    }
}
```

3. **Inter-Service Communication for Authorization**

Other services, such as an order service or profile service, can call the authentication service's /auth/validate endpoint to verify a user's identity. For efficiency, services may use Spring WebClient or Feign to communicate with the authentication service.

Conclusion

Microservices architecture enables Java applications to scale independently, improve fault tolerance, and support rapid development cycles. Using Spring Boot makes microservice development simpler and more manageable, offering powerful tools for building, deploying, and scaling services. In this chapter, we explored the core principles of microservices, addressed inter-service communication and data consistency, and demonstrated how to implement a scalable user authentication microservice.

By mastering microservices design, Java developers can build applications that handle high traffic, adapt to changing requirements, and provide robust services across distributed environments. As you continue, these principles will be key to building efficient, scalable, and maintainable applications.

Chapter 8: Design Patterns for Scalable Java Applications

Design patterns are essential for building scalable, maintainable, and efficient Java applications, especially in complex systems. They provide solutions to recurring problems in software design, promoting best practices and making code easier to extend and adapt. In this chapter, we'll explore key design patterns that support scalability in Java applications, with a focus on patterns for distributed and event-driven architectures. We'll conclude with a practical example implementing the Observer pattern to create a notification system in an event-driven application.

Key Design Patterns for Scalable Applications

Scalable Java applications require thoughtful design to manage complexity, support high traffic, and handle large datasets efficiently. Design patterns help in organizing code, managing dependencies, and ensuring that the application can handle increasing loads without compromising performance. Here are some of the most effective patterns for building scalable applications.

1. Singleton Pattern

The Singleton pattern ensures that a class has only one instance and provides a global access point to it. This pattern is particularly useful in applications where a single resource, such as a database connection or configuration manager, needs to be shared across multiple classes.

- **Use Case**: A database connection pool where a single instance manages and provides connections.

Implementation:

```
public class DatabaseConnection {
    private static DatabaseConnection instance;

    private DatabaseConnection() {}

    public static synchronized DatabaseConnection getInstance() {
        if (instance == null) {
            instance = new DatabaseConnection();
        }
```

```
        return instance;

    }

}
```

In this implementation, DatabaseConnection is created once and reused throughout the application, reducing memory usage and avoiding redundant connections.

2. Factory Pattern

The Factory pattern provides a way to create objects without specifying the exact class. This pattern is beneficial in scalable applications where objects of different types are needed based on specific criteria.

- **Use Case**: Creating different types of payment processors (e.g., PayPal, Stripe, Credit Card) based on the payment method selected.

Implementation:

```
public class PaymentFactory {

    public static PaymentProcessor getProcessor(String type) {

        switch (type) {

            case "PayPal":

                return new PayPalProcessor();

            case "CreditCard":
```

```
            return new CreditCardProcessor();

        default:

            throw new
IllegalArgumentException("Invalid payment type");

        }

    }

}
```

Using a factory decouples the client code from specific implementations, improving flexibility and scalability as new payment methods can be added without changing the client code.

3. Proxy Pattern

The Proxy pattern acts as a placeholder or intermediary for another object, often to control access or add functionality. In distributed applications, proxies are useful for caching, logging, or lazy loading resources.

- **Use Case**: Caching data to reduce the number of network requests, such as using a proxy for a database or remote API.

Implementation:

```
public class DataProxy implements DataService {

    private DataService dataService;
```

```java
    private Map<String, Data> cache = new
HashMap<>();

    public Data getData(String id) {
        if (cache.containsKey(id)) {
            return cache.get(id);
        }
        Data data = dataService.getData(id);
        cache.put(id, data);
        return data;
    }
}
```

The DataProxy caches results from dataService, reducing repeated database or network calls and enhancing performance in a high-traffic application.

Design Patterns for Distributed Systems

Distributed systems present unique challenges, such as managing communication between services, handling failure, and maintaining data consistency. Certain design patterns are particularly well-suited to address these challenges in distributed Java applications.

1. Circuit Breaker Pattern

The Circuit Breaker pattern helps prevent a system from making requests to a failing service, reducing the load on that service and allowing it to recover. This pattern is particularly valuable in distributed systems, where a single failing service can degrade overall system performance.

- **Use Case**: Prevent repeated calls to an unavailable database or external API.

Implementation:

```java
public class CircuitBreaker {
    private boolean open = false;
    private int failureCount = 0;
    private final int threshold = 3;

    public void callService() {
        if (open) {
            throw new IllegalStateException("Circuit breaker is open.");
        }
```

```
try {
    // Attempt service call
} catch (Exception e) {
    failureCount++;
    if (failureCount >= threshold) {
        open = true;
    }
}
}


public void reset() {
    open = false;
    failureCount = 0;
}
}
```

If the failure count reaches a certain threshold, the circuit breaker opens, preventing further calls until it's reset, ensuring that system resources are not wasted on failed requests.

2. Service Registry Pattern

In a distributed system, services need to locate each other dynamically. The Service Registry pattern involves maintaining a registry of service instances, allowing services to discover others.

- **Use Case**: Service discovery in a microservices architecture, where services are registered dynamically and accessed through a registry.

Spring Cloud provides Eureka, a service registry implementation that allows services to register themselves and discover others.

Design Patterns for Event-Driven Architecture

Event-driven architectures are increasingly common in scalable applications, allowing services to react to events asynchronously, promoting loose coupling and resilience.

1. Observer Pattern

The Observer pattern is a key pattern in event-driven architectures. It involves a subject that maintains a list of observers and notifies them of any state changes. This pattern is useful for applications where multiple components need to react to changes in a central component.

- **Use Case**: Sending notifications to users when certain events occur, such as order confirmation, shipment updates, or account activity.

Implementation:

```
public interface Observer {

    void update(String event);

}
```

```
public class NotificationService implements Observer {

    public void update(String event) {

        System.out.println("Notification sent: " + event);

    }

}
```

```
public class EventPublisher {

    private List<Observer> observers = new ArrayList<>();
```

```java
public void registerObserver(Observer observer) {
    observers.add(observer);
}

public void notifyObservers(String event) {
    for (Observer observer : observers) {
        observer.update(event);
    }
}
}
```

In this example, the EventPublisher notifies all registered observers when an event occurs, allowing them to take action independently.

Scenario: Implementing the Observer Pattern for Event-Driven Notifications

Let's explore a scenario where we implement the Observer pattern to create a notification system for an e-commerce platform. The system will send notifications to customers when specific events occur, such as order confirmation, shipping updates, and delivery confirmations.

Problem Statement

In an e-commerce application, users should receive notifications at different stages of their order lifecycle. To ensure scalability and maintainability, the notification system should be loosely coupled with other services, so that notifications can be added or modified without impacting other components.

Solution Design Using the Observer Pattern

1. Define the Subject and Observer

The OrderService acts as the subject, publishing events when orders are confirmed, shipped, or delivered. The NotificationService is the observer, reacting to these events and sending notifications.

Code for Observer Interface and Notification Service:

```java
public interface Observer {
    void update(String event);
}


public class NotificationService implements Observer {
```

```java
    @Override
    public void update(String event) {
        System.out.println("Notification sent: " + event);
    }
}
```

2. Create the Event Publisher (Subject)

The OrderService will act as the publisher of events. When an order is updated, it notifies all observers (in this case, NotificationService) to trigger a notification.

```java
public class OrderService {
    private List<Observer> observers = new ArrayList<>();

    public void registerObserver(Observer observer) {
        observers.add(observer);
    }

    public void notifyObservers(String event) {
        for (Observer observer : observers) {
            observer.update(event);
        }
```

```
}
```

```java
    public void updateOrderStatus(String orderId, String
status) {

        // Logic to update order status

        notifyObservers("Order " + orderId + " status: " +
status);

    }
}
```

3. Integrate and Test the Notification System

When an order is updated, the OrderService triggers a notification to all registered observers, ensuring that users receive updates without tightly coupling notification logic to order processing.

Example Usage:

```java
public class Main {
    public static void main(String[] args) {

        OrderService orderService = new OrderService();

        NotificationService notificationService = new
NotificationService();
```

```
orderService.registerObserver(notificationService);
```

```
// Update order status, triggering notifications
orderService.updateOrderStatus("12345",
"Confirmed");
orderService.updateOrderStatus("12345",
"Shipped");
    }
}
```

This setup allows the OrderService to notify
NotificationService independently, and additional
services can be added as observers if needed, such as
SMS notifications or email notifications, without
modifying the core order processing logic.

Conclusion

Design patterns are foundational to building scalable,
maintainable, and resilient Java applications,
especially in complex, distributed, and event-driven
systems. In this chapter, we covered core design
patterns for scalability, including the Singleton,
Factory, and Proxy patterns. We explored patterns for
distributed systems like Circuit Breaker and Service
Registry, which help manage fault tolerance, service
discovery, and performance. Additionally, we

discussed the Observer pattern, a critical pattern in event-driven systems, and implemented it in a scenario for creating a notification system.

Mastering design patterns enables Java developers to tackle complex architectural challenges, design systems that scale, and create applications that are adaptable to changing requirements. As you build more sophisticated applications, these patterns will serve as essential tools for addressing common problems in scalable software design.

Chapter 9: Event-Driven and Reactive Programming

In a world where applications need to handle massive amounts of data, process requests instantly, and remain responsive under heavy load, traditional programming paradigms can fall short. Event-driven and reactive programming have become essential approaches for building responsive, resilient, and scalable applications. This chapter explores the principles of reactive programming with tools like Project Reactor and RxJava, shows how non-blocking I/O contributes to responsiveness, and concludes with a practical example of building a real-time stock trading application.

Principles of Reactive Programming

Reactive programming is an asynchronous programming paradigm centered around data streams and the propagation of change. It allows applications to react to events as they occur, without blocking resources. The goal is to build applications that are **responsive**, **resilient**, **elastic**, and **message-driven**—

qualities often summarized by the **Reactive Manifesto**.

1. Core Principles of Reactive Programming

1. **Responsive**: Reactive applications respond to events in real time. They are designed to provide consistent and fast responses, even under varying loads.

2. **Resilient**: By isolating and handling failure gracefully, reactive systems can recover from errors without compromising the entire application. Resilience is achieved through fallback mechanisms and error handling.

3. **Elastic**: Reactive systems scale as demand increases, distributing load across multiple instances and resources to handle fluctuations efficiently.

4. **Message-Driven**: Communication between components is asynchronous and event-based, allowing different parts of the system to work independently and send or receive messages as needed.

Reactive programming frameworks, like Project Reactor and RxJava, help manage asynchronous data flows, making it easier to process streams of data in real time.

Introduction to Project Reactor and RxJava

Project Reactor and **RxJava** are two popular Java frameworks for building reactive applications. They offer tools for handling asynchronous data streams and provide a range of operators for transforming, filtering, and aggregating data.

Project Reactor

Project Reactor is a reactive programming library for building non-blocking applications in Java. It is based on the **Reactive Streams specification**, which provides a standard for asynchronous stream processing. Reactor's key building blocks are Mono and Flux:

- **Mono**: Represents a single asynchronous result, such as a single HTTP response or database query result.

- **Flux**: Represents a sequence of asynchronous elements, useful for streaming data like stock price updates or user actions.

Example of Mono and Flux:

```
import reactor.core.publisher.Mono;

import reactor.core.publisher.Flux;
```

```
Mono<String> singleResponse = Mono.just("Hello,
Reactor!");
```

```
Flux<String> multipleResponses = Flux.just("Hello",
"Reactor", "World");
```

Reactor supports backpressure, a mechanism that allows the consumer to control the rate of data production, ensuring that resources are used efficiently.

RxJava

RxJava is a library for composing asynchronous and event-based programs using observable sequences. It is based on the **Observer pattern** and provides a wide range of operators to transform, combine, and filter data streams. The primary types in RxJava are Observable and Single:

- **Observable**: Emits a sequence of items, similar to Reactor's Flux.

- **Single**: Emits a single item or error, similar to Reactor's Mono.

Example of Observable and Single:

```
import io.reactivex.rxjava3.core.Observable;

import io.reactivex.rxjava3.core.Single;
```

```
Single<String> singleResult = Single.just("Hello,
RxJava!");
```

```
Observable<String> multipleResults =
Observable.just("Hello", "RxJava", "World");
```

Both Project Reactor and RxJava allow developers to handle complex asynchronous tasks with ease, supporting operators for mapping, filtering, combining, and aggregating data streams.

Creating Responsive, Resilient Applications with Non-Blocking I/O

Non-blocking I/O enables applications to handle multiple requests simultaneously without blocking a thread for each request. This is crucial in reactive programming, where the goal is to maximize resource utilization by allowing threads to handle multiple tasks in parallel.

How Non-Blocking I/O Works

Traditional I/O operations are blocking, meaning a thread remains occupied until the operation completes. In contrast, non-blocking I/O allows threads to initiate an operation and continue processing other tasks while waiting for the result. This approach improves efficiency, especially in applications that handle high volumes of network requests or file I/O.

Non-blocking I/O is essential in building reactive applications because it enables:

- **Increased Throughput**: By freeing up threads to process other tasks, non-blocking I/O enables the system to handle more requests concurrently.

- **Reduced Latency**: Non-blocking operations reduce waiting times, making the application more responsive.

- **Improved Scalability**: Applications can handle more connections with fewer threads, reducing resource consumption and improving scalability.

Java's NIO (Non-blocking I/O) package and asynchronous libraries like Project Reactor and RxJava make it easier to implement non-blocking operations in Java applications.

Reactive and Non-Blocking HTTP Requests with WebClient

Spring WebClient is a reactive, non-blocking HTTP client for making HTTP requests in Java applications. It is commonly used with Project Reactor to create non-blocking API calls.

Example of Using WebClient with Project Reactor:

```java
import
org.springframework.web.reactive.function.client.Web
Client;

import reactor.core.publisher.Mono;


WebClient webClient =
WebClient.create("https://api.stock.com");


Mono<String> response = webClient.get()

    .uri("/stockPrice")

    .retrieve()

    .bodyToMono(String.class);


response.subscribe(System.out::println);
```

In this example, WebClient retrieves data from an external API without blocking the main thread, enabling the application to handle other tasks while waiting for the response.

Practical Example: Real-Time Stock Trading Application

Let's build a practical example to demonstrate how reactive programming can be used in a real-time stock trading application. In this application, we'll use Project Reactor to create a reactive pipeline that processes live stock price updates and executes buy or sell trades based on predefined conditions.

Problem Statement

The stock trading application needs to:

1. Continuously listen to real-time stock price updates from an API.

2. Process each price update as it arrives.

3. Automatically execute buy or sell trades based on trading rules (e.g., buy when price is below a threshold, sell when price exceeds a threshold).

To achieve this, we'll use Project Reactor's Flux to handle the stream of stock prices and apply reactive operators to manage trades in a non-blocking, asynchronous manner.

Solution Using Project Reactor

   1. **Set Up the Stock Price Stream**

In this scenario, we'll simulate a stream of stock prices using a Flux, but in a real application, this data would come from an external API.

```java
import reactor.core.publisher.Flux;

import java.time.Duration;

import java.util.Random;


public class StockPriceGenerator {


    public static Flux<Double> getPriceStream() {

        Random random = new Random();

        return Flux.interval(Duration.ofSeconds(1))

                .map(i -> 100 + random.nextDouble() * 10);
        // Simulate price range between 100 and 110

    }

}
```

The getPriceStream method generates random stock prices every second, creating a simulated real-time price stream.

2. **Define the Trading Rules**

Next, we define a TradingService that subscribes to the price stream and executes trades based on predefined rules.

java

```java
public class TradingService {

    private static final double BUY_THRESHOLD = 102.0;

    private static final double SELL_THRESHOLD = 108.0;


    public void processTrades() {
        StockPriceGenerator.getPriceStream()
            .doOnNext(price ->
System.out.println("Current Price: $" + price))
            .filter(price -> price < BUY_THRESHOLD
|| price > SELL_THRESHOLD)
            .subscribe(price -> {
                if (price < BUY_THRESHOLD) {
                    System.out.println("Executing BUY
order at $" + price);
                } else if (price > SELL_THRESHOLD) {
                    System.out.println("Executing SELL
order at $" + price);
                }
            });
```

```
    }
}
```

In this example, processTrades subscribes to the price stream. For each price, it checks whether the price is below the buy threshold or above the sell threshold. If the condition is met, it executes a buy or sell trade accordingly.

3. **Handling Errors and Resilience**

In a real application, external data sources may experience temporary failures. Reactive programming makes it easy to handle such scenarios using error-handling operators.

```
public void processTradesWithErrorHandling() {

    StockPriceGenerator.getPriceStream()

        .doOnNext(price ->
System.out.println("Current Price: $" + price))

        .filter(price -> price < BUY_THRESHOLD ||
price > SELL_THRESHOLD)

        .doOnError(error -> System.out.println("Error
in data stream: " + error.getMessage()))

        .retry(3) // Retry up to 3 times on error

        .subscribe(price -> {
```

```java
            if (price < BUY_THRESHOLD) {

                System.out.println("Executing BUY order
at $" + price);

                } else if (price > SELL_THRESHOLD) {

                System.out.println("Executing SELL
order at $" + price);

                }

            });

    }
```

Here, doOnError logs any errors in the price stream, and retry(3) retries up to three times if an error occurs, enhancing resilience.

4. Testing the Reactive Trading Application

Finally, we run the application and observe the output.

```java
public class Main {

    public static void main(String[] args) {

        TradingService tradingService = new
TradingService();

tradingService.processTradesWithErrorHandling();

    }

}
```

The program continuously monitors stock prices and executes trades based on the rules, logging any errors and retrying as needed. This approach creates a highly responsive, resilient application that can handle real-time data streams efficiently.

Conclusion

Event-driven and reactive programming offer powerful tools for creating responsive, resilient applications that handle real-time data streams and large volumes of requests efficiently. This chapter covered the core principles of reactive programming, introduced Project Reactor and RxJava as tools for handling asynchronous data, and showed how non-blocking I/O enhances scalability and responsiveness.

Through the example of a real-time stock trading application, we demonstrated how to set up reactive pipelines, process real-time data, and handle errors gracefully. By mastering these techniques, Java developers can build applications that respond instantly to events, scale seamlessly under load, and remain resilient in the face of failures, making them well-suited for today's demanding applications.

Part 3
Java for High-Performance Applications

Chapter 10: Performance Tuning and Optimization

Performance tuning and optimization are crucial in building Java applications that handle high traffic, process large amounts of data, and deliver results with minimal latency. Even well-written code can suffer from bottlenecks that limit throughput, increase memory usage, and slow down execution. In this chapter, we'll explore profiling tools for identifying performance bottlenecks, techniques for optimizing code efficiency, and apply these principles to a high-throughput data pipeline.

Profiling Tools for Identifying Bottlenecks

Profiling is the process of measuring an application's resource usage—such as CPU, memory, and I/O—during execution. Profiling tools help identify bottlenecks and inefficient code sections, providing data to guide optimization efforts.

1. VisualVM

VisualVM is a powerful, open-source tool that provides detailed insights into CPU usage, memory allocation, and thread activity. It integrates with the Java Development Kit (JDK) and provides an easy-to-use GUI for monitoring Java applications in real time.

- **CPU Profiling**: VisualVM's CPU profiler identifies which methods consume the most processing time, helping you focus on optimizing CPU-intensive parts.

- **Memory Profiling**: Tracks memory usage, including objects that take up the most space, aiding in identifying potential memory leaks.

- **Heap Dump Analysis**: VisualVM can capture heap dumps, allowing you to analyze object allocations and pinpoint memory issues.

Example Usage: Start your application and open it in VisualVM. Use the CPU profiler to identify any methods with high CPU consumption and the memory profiler to look for excessive object allocations or potential memory leaks.

2. JProfiler

JProfiler is a comprehensive, commercial profiling tool that offers deep insights into application performance. It provides more detailed and advanced features than VisualVM, making it a popular choice for enterprise Java applications.

- **CPU and Memory Profiling**: Similar to VisualVM but with more detailed breakdowns and the ability to drill down into classes and methods.

- **Database and I/O Profiling**: Tracks database queries and I/O operations, enabling optimization of database access and I/O performance.

- **Thread Profiling**: Allows developers to view thread activity and identify potential deadlocks or high-thread contention.

Example Usage: Run the profiler on a test environment, execute common workflows, and analyze thread, CPU, and memory usage. Look for high-frequency methods or memory-hogging data structures to optimize.

3. Java Flight Recorder (JFR)

Java Flight Recorder (JFR), built into the JDK since Java 11, records low-level information about your application's behavior, such as method calls, memory allocations, and I/O events.

- **Low Overhead**: JFR runs with minimal impact on performance, making it suitable for production environments.

- **Detailed Event Recording**: Captures information about garbage collection, CPU usage, memory allocation, and thread activity.

- **Customizable**: JFR allows you to configure which events to record, tailoring the profiler to your application's needs.

Example Usage: Start a JFR session for a specific task and analyze the recordings to identify bottlenecks and high CPU or memory usage.

Techniques for Code Efficiency

Efficient code is essential for high-performance applications. Optimizing code can reduce CPU usage, minimize memory allocation, and improve application responsiveness. Here are key optimization techniques to enhance code efficiency.

1. Inlining

Inlining is an optimization technique where the Java compiler replaces a method call with the method's body. This eliminates the overhead of calling the method, reducing execution time. The Just-In-Time (JIT) compiler automatically inlines small methods, but you can encourage inlining by keeping frequently called methods short and efficient.

- **Manual Inlining**: For small helper methods that are frequently called, consider replacing the method call with inline code. However, avoid excessive inlining, as it can lead to bloated code.

- **JIT Optimization**: The JIT compiler performs automatic inlining, particularly on methods that are frequently executed in tight loops. Keeping critical methods small increases the likelihood of inlining.

Example:

```
public class MathOperations {
   public int square(int x) {
      return x * x;
   }
}
```

```
// Inline usage
int result = x * x; // Instead of
mathOperations.square(x);
```

2. Loop Unrolling

Loop unrolling is a technique where the loop body is expanded, reducing the number of iterations and minimizing loop overhead. This optimization works well for loops with a fixed number of iterations.

Example:

```
// Original loop
for (int i = 0; i < 4; i++) {
    sum += array[i];
}


// Unrolled loop
sum += array[0];
sum += array[1];
sum += array[2];
sum += array[3];
```

Loop unrolling reduces the overhead of incrementing i and checking loop conditions, which can lead to performance gains in tight loops, though it should be used carefully as it increases code size.

3. Reducing Object Allocation

Reducing object allocation can significantly improve performance, as excessive allocation and deallocation consume memory and trigger frequent garbage collection. Aim to reuse objects, avoid unnecessary object creation, and prefer primitives over wrapper classes where possible.

- **Object Reuse**: Use object pooling or caching for frequently used objects, such as database connections or reusable data structures.

- **Use Primitives**: Prefer int, double, and other primitives over wrapper classes like Integer or Double for basic calculations.

Example:

```
// Unnecessary allocation
Integer sum = new Integer(0);
```

```
// Optimized with primitive type
int sum = 0;
```

4. String Optimization

Strings in Java are immutable, and creating multiple copies of strings can lead to high memory usage. Use StringBuilder for string concatenation within loops and avoid repetitive string operations where possible.

Example:

```
// Inefficient string concatenation in a loop
String result = "";
```

```java
for (String s : strings) {
    result += s;
}


// Optimized with StringBuilder
StringBuilder result = new StringBuilder();
for (String s : strings) {
    result.append(s);
}
```

StringBuilder minimizes memory allocation by modifying the buffer in place, making it significantly faster than concatenating strings.

5. Avoiding Reflection and Dynamic Class Loading

Reflection and dynamic class loading are useful for flexibility but can be slow and memory-intensive. Minimize their use, especially in performance-sensitive sections of code.

Scenario: Optimizing a High-Throughput Data Pipeline

Let's walk through a practical example of optimizing a high-throughput data pipeline. In this scenario, we have a Java application that processes large volumes of data records from a source, performs calculations, and stores results in a database. We'll use profiling tools to identify bottlenecks, apply optimization techniques, and improve the pipeline's performance.

Problem Statement

The data pipeline processes 1,000 records per second and applies complex calculations to each record. However, the pipeline struggles to keep up with high input rates, causing delays and increasing memory usage. Our goal is to optimize the pipeline to handle higher throughput while reducing CPU and memory usage.

Solution: Applying Profiling and Optimization Techniques

1. Profiling the Data Pipeline

First, we use JProfiler to identify performance bottlenecks in the data pipeline. Here are some initial observations:

- **CPU Bottleneck**: The profiling results show that a method called processData() consumes a significant portion of CPU time.

- **Memory Allocation**: The profiler identifies high memory usage in string concatenation operations within a loop.

- o **Frequent Garbage Collection**: Frequent object allocation triggers garbage collection frequently, slowing down the application.

2. **Optimizing CPU Usage with Inlining and Loop Unrolling**

The processData() method performs multiple calculations within a loop, where small helper methods are called repeatedly. By inlining these helper methods and unrolling the loop, we can reduce CPU overhead.

Original Code:

```java
public void processData(List<Data> records) {
    for (Data record : records) {
        int result = calculate(record);
        storeResult(result);
    }
}


private int calculate(Data record) {
    return record.getValue() * 2; // Example calculation
}
```

Optimized Code:

```java
public void processData(List<Data> records) {

    for (Data record : records) {

        int result = record.getValue() * 2; // Inlined
calculation

        storeResult(result);

    }

}
```

By inlining calculate(), we eliminate the method call overhead, and loop unrolling (if applicable) would further reduce CPU usage.

3. **Reducing Memory Allocation**

Memory profiling shows that strings are heavily allocated within the loop. We replace repetitive string concatenation with StringBuilder to minimize memory allocation.

Original Code:

```java
public void logResults(List<Data> records) {

    String resultLog = "";

    for (Data record : records) {
```

```
        resultLog += record.getId() + ",";

    }

}
```

Optimized Code:

```
public void logResults(List<Data> records) {

    StringBuilder resultLog = new StringBuilder();

    for (Data record : records) {

        resultLog.append(record.getId()).append(",");

    }

}
```

By using StringBuilder, we reduce unnecessary string object creation, which decreases memory usage and reduces garbage collection frequency.

4. Optimizing Database Access with Batch Processing

The profiler shows that individual database inserts are causing I/O delays. By batching database operations, we reduce the number of I/O operations and improve throughput.

Original Code:

```java
public void storeResult(int result) {

    database.insert(result); // Individual insert

}
```

Optimized Code:

```java
public void storeResultsBatch(List<Integer> results) {

    database.insertBatch(results); // Batch insert

}
```

By performing batch inserts, we minimize the number of database calls, leading to reduced I/O wait times and higher overall throughput.

5. **Using Non-Blocking I/O for Scalability**

To make the pipeline more resilient under high loads, we can use non-blocking I/O, allowing other tasks to continue while waiting for data processing.

```java
import java.util.concurrent.CompletableFuture;


public void processDataAsync(List<Data> records) {

    CompletableFuture.runAsync(() ->
processData(records));
```

}

Non-blocking I/O enables the application to process multiple batches concurrently, improving scalability and responsiveness.

Conclusion

Performance tuning and optimization are essential for building scalable, high-performance applications. This chapter covered profiling tools like VisualVM, JProfiler, and Java Flight Recorder to identify bottlenecks, as well as optimization techniques like inlining, loop unrolling, and memory allocation reduction to improve code efficiency.

Through a practical scenario of optimizing a high-throughput data pipeline, we demonstrated how to apply these techniques to real-world applications. By mastering these tools and techniques, Java developers can build applications that handle high traffic and large datasets while maintaining responsiveness and resource efficiency.

Chapter 11: Advanced Java I/O for High Performance

High-performance I/O is critical for applications that handle large volumes of data, process files, or manage real-time communication. Java's traditional I/O (Input/Output) model, known as Java IO, provides simple I/O operations but can be inefficient for high-performance requirements due to its blocking nature. Java NIO (Non-blocking I/O) and asynchronous processing allow applications to perform I/O operations more efficiently by taking advantage of non-blocking, direct memory access, and asynchronous capabilities. In this chapter, we'll explore Java NIO, memory-mapped files, file channels, and streaming optimizations, concluding with a real-world example of building efficient I/O for a real-time messaging application.

Java NIO and Asynchronous Data Processing

Java NIO (New I/O), introduced in Java 1.4, provides a powerful alternative to traditional Java IO. NIO is designed for high-performance applications that require efficient I/O operations, particularly for network communication and file processing. Java NIO is built around three key components: **buffers**, **channels**, and **selectors**, enabling non-blocking I/O and asynchronous data processing.

1. Buffers and Channels

In Java NIO, **buffers** are containers that store data in memory, while **channels** provide a direct connection to I/O sources, such as files or sockets. This structure enables more efficient data handling by minimizing the overhead of copying data between user space and kernel space.

- **Buffer**: Buffers are used to hold data while it's being read from or written to channels. They support various data types, including ByteBuffer, CharBuffer, and IntBuffer.

Example of ByteBuffer Usage:

java

```
ByteBuffer buffer = ByteBuffer.allocate(1024);
```

```java
buffer.put("Hello, NIO".getBytes());
buffer.flip(); // Prepare for reading
while (buffer.hasRemaining()) {
    System.out.print((char) buffer.get());
}
```

- **Channel**: Channels represent connections to I/O sources and destinations, such as files or network sockets. Channels work with buffers to enable non-blocking data transfer.

Example of FileChannel Usage:

```java
try (RandomAccessFile file = new RandomAccessFile("data.txt", "rw");
    FileChannel channel = file.getChannel()) {
    ByteBuffer buffer = ByteBuffer.allocate(1024);
    int bytesRead = channel.read(buffer);
    while (bytesRead != -1) {
        buffer.flip();
        while (buffer.hasRemaining()) {
            System.out.print((char) buffer.get());
        }
```

```
    buffer.clear();

    bytesRead = channel.read(buffer);

  }

} catch (IOException e) {

  e.printStackTrace();

}
```

In this example, FileChannel reads data into a buffer, and we process the buffer's contents in a non-blocking manner.

2. Selectors and Non-blocking I/O

Selectors allow a single thread to manage multiple channels, making it possible to handle multiple connections without blocking. In a typical non-blocking setup, a single thread continuously checks for ready channels and processes data without waiting for I/O operations to complete.

- **Non-blocking Mode**: Channels can be set to non-blocking mode, where operations like read() and write() don't block the thread. If no data is available, the thread can perform other tasks.

- **Selector**: A Selector checks for channels that are ready for specific operations (like reading or writing) and enables event-driven processing.

Example of Selector Usage:

```java
try (Selector selector = Selector.open();

    ServerSocketChannel serverSocketChannel =
ServerSocketChannel.open()) {

    serverSocketChannel.configureBlocking(false);

    serverSocketChannel.bind(new
InetSocketAddress(8080));

    serverSocketChannel.register(selector,
SelectionKey.OP_ACCEPT);


    while (true) {

        selector.select();

        Set<SelectionKey> selectedKeys =
selector.selectedKeys();

        for (SelectionKey key : selectedKeys) {

            if (key.isAcceptable()) {

                SocketChannel client =
serverSocketChannel.accept();

                client.configureBlocking(false);

                client.register(selector,
SelectionKey.OP_READ);

            } else if (key.isReadable()) {
```

```java
        SocketChannel client = (SocketChannel)
key.channel();

        ByteBuffer buffer =
ByteBuffer.allocate(1024);

        client.read(buffer);

        buffer.flip();

        System.out.println("Received message: " +
new String(buffer.array()).trim());

        }

    }

    selectedKeys.clear();

  }

} catch (IOException e) {

  e.printStackTrace();

}
```

This example shows how a single thread manages multiple client connections using a Selector, efficiently handling I/O without blocking.

3. Asynchronous Channels

Java NIO.2 (introduced in Java 7) further extended NIO by adding asynchronous channels for file and socket I/O. Asynchronous channels allow I/O operations to be executed in the background, freeing up the main thread for other tasks. These channels are particularly useful in high-throughput systems where non-blocking I/O alone isn't enough.

Example of AsynchronousFileChannel Usage:

```java
Path path = Paths.get("data.txt");

AsynchronousFileChannel asyncChannel =
AsynchronousFileChannel.open(path,
StandardOpenOption.READ);

ByteBuffer buffer = ByteBuffer.allocate(1024);

asyncChannel.read(buffer, 0, buffer, new
CompletionHandler<Integer, ByteBuffer>() {

    @Override
    public void completed(Integer result, ByteBuffer
attachment) {

        attachment.flip();

        System.out.println("Read data: " + new
String(attachment.array()));

    }


    @Override
    public void failed(Throwable exc, ByteBuffer
attachment) {
```

```
    System.err.println("Read failed: " +
exc.getMessage());

    }
});
```

In this example, AsynchronousFileChannel reads data asynchronously, allowing the main thread to continue without waiting for I/O completion.

Memory-Mapped Files, File Channels, and Streaming Optimizations

Memory-mapped files, file channels, and streaming optimizations are additional techniques for achieving high-performance I/O, especially for large files or streaming applications.

1. Memory-Mapped Files

Memory-mapped files allow portions of a file to be mapped directly into memory, enabling fast access to large files without reading them fully into memory. Java NIO provides MappedByteBuffer for creating memory-mapped files, ideal for handling large datasets.

Example of Memory-Mapped File Usage:

```
try (RandomAccessFile file = new
RandomAccessFile("largefile.dat", "rw");
    FileChannel channel = file.getChannel()) {
    MappedByteBuffer buffer =
channel.map(FileChannel.MapMode.READ_WRITE,
0, channel.size());
    for (int i = 0; i < buffer.limit(); i++) {
        buffer.put((byte) (buffer.get(i) + 1)); // Example
modification
    }
} catch (IOException e) {
    e.printStackTrace();
}
```

Memory-mapped files are ideal for applications requiring fast access to large files, such as databases or video streaming.

2. File Channels and Direct Buffers

File channels provide high-performance file I/O by enabling direct access to file data through channels and buffers. File channels are particularly effective when combined with **direct buffers**, which allocate memory outside the JVM heap and reduce garbage collection.

Example of Direct Buffer Usage:

```java
try (FileChannel channel =
FileChannel.open(Paths.get("data.bin"),
StandardOpenOption.READ)) {

    ByteBuffer buffer =
ByteBuffer.allocateDirect(1024); // Direct buffer

    int bytesRead = channel.read(buffer);

    buffer.flip();

    while (buffer.hasRemaining()) {

        System.out.print((char) buffer.get());

    }
} catch (IOException e) {

    e.printStackTrace();

}
```

Direct buffers enable faster I/O operations and reduce the need for memory copying between the JVM and the operating system, improving performance for I/O-intensive applications.

3. Streaming Optimizations

Streaming is essential for real-time and large-scale applications that process continuous data. Java provides several techniques for optimizing streaming, including:

- **Buffered Streams**: BufferedInputStream and BufferedOutputStream reduce the number of read and write operations by buffering data in memory, which speeds up I/O operations.

- **Pipeline Processing**: Using streams as a pipeline allows applications to process data as it arrives, improving throughput and latency.

Example of Buffered Streaming:

```
try (BufferedInputStream in = new
BufferedInputStream(new
FileInputStream("data.txt"));

    BufferedOutputStream out = new
BufferedOutputStream(new
FileOutputStream("output.txt"))) {

  byte[] buffer = new byte[1024];

  int bytesRead;

  while ((bytesRead = in.read(buffer)) != -1) {

    out.write(buffer, 0, bytesRead);

  }
```

```
} catch (IOException e) {

    e.printStackTrace();

}
```

Buffered streaming is useful for reading and writing large files or data streams, minimizing the number of I/O operations and improving performance.

Example: Efficient I/O for Real-Time Messaging Application

Let's create a real-time messaging application that efficiently processes high volumes of messages using Java NIO and asynchronous processing.

Problem Statement

The messaging application needs to handle a high volume of real-time messages between multiple clients. The requirements are:

1. Efficiently handle multiple client connections without blocking.

2. Process incoming messages and broadcast them to all connected clients.

3. Optimize resource usage to support high concurrency.

Solution Using Java NIO with Asynchronous I/O

1. **Setting Up Non-Blocking ServerSocketChannel**

We use ServerSocketChannel in non-blocking mode to accept client connections without blocking the server thread.

```
try (ServerSocketChannel serverChannel =
ServerSocketChannel.open()) {

    serverChannel.bind(new InetSocketAddress(9090));

    serverChannel.configureBlocking(false);

    Selector selector = Selector.open();

    serverChannel.register(selector,
SelectionKey.OP_ACCEPT);
} catch (IOException e) {

    e.printStackTrace();

}
```

2. **Handling Client Connections with Selector**

We use a Selector to manage multiple client connections. When a new message arrives, it's read from the client's SocketChannel and then broadcasted to all other clients.

```java
Set<SocketChannel> clients =
ConcurrentHashMap.newKeySet();


while (true) {

    selector.select();

    Set<SelectionKey> selectedKeys =
selector.selectedKeys();

    for (SelectionKey key : selectedKeys) {

        if (key.isAcceptable()) {

            SocketChannel clientChannel =
serverChannel.accept();

            clientChannel.configureBlocking(false);

            clientChannel.register(selector,
SelectionKey.OP_READ);

            clients.add(clientChannel);

        } else if (key.isReadable()) {

            SocketChannel clientChannel =
(SocketChannel) key.channel();

            ByteBuffer buffer = ByteBuffer.allocate(1024);

            int bytesRead = clientChannel.read(buffer);

            if (bytesRead > 0) {
```

```
        buffer.flip();

        broadcastMessage(buffer, clientChannel);

      }

    }

  }

  selectedKeys.clear();

}
```

3. Broadcasting Messages to All Clients

The broadcastMessage method sends each message to all connected clients, ensuring efficient non-blocking message broadcasting.

```
private void broadcastMessage(ByteBuffer buffer,
SocketChannel sender) {

  for (SocketChannel client : clients) {

    if (client != sender) {

      try {

        client.write(buffer.duplicate());

      } catch (IOException e) {

        clients.remove(client);

      }

    }
```

```
        }

    }
```

4. Running the Real-Time Messaging Application

The application continuously processes messages from multiple clients, broadcasting each message in real time. This setup ensures efficient handling of multiple connections, high message throughput, and low latency.

Conclusion

Advanced Java I/O techniques enable developers to build high-performance applications that efficiently handle large volumes of data, real-time communication, and resource-intensive operations. In this chapter, we covered Java NIO and asynchronous processing, explored memory-mapped files and direct buffers, and implemented efficient streaming techniques.

Through the real-time messaging application example, we demonstrated how to use non-blocking I/O and selectors to build a responsive, scalable system. Mastering these I/O techniques is essential for developing Java applications that meet today's demanding performance requirements.

Chapter 12: Serialization and Deserialization in Java

Serialization and deserialization are critical techniques for data exchange in distributed systems. They allow objects to be converted into a format that can be easily transferred over a network, stored in a file, or cached in memory, and then reconstructed (deserialized) back into objects. Serialization is essential for high-performance applications that rely on efficient data transfer between services, particularly in microservices, RESTful APIs, and real-time systems. This chapter explores serialization techniques, including Protocol Buffers, Avro, and custom serialization methods, and demonstrates these principles in a case study focusing on high-performance APIs.

Serialization Techniques for Optimized Data Transfer

Serialization involves converting an object into a byte stream or another format, which can be transported over a network or stored in a file. Java provides several serialization methods, each suited to different use cases, based on efficiency, compatibility, and format flexibility.

1. Java's Built-In Serialization

Java's built-in serialization mechanism uses the Serializable interface to convert objects into byte streams, which can be stored or transmitted. This approach is simple but can be inefficient in terms of performance and byte size, making it less suitable for high-performance systems.

- **How It Works**: Classes implement the Serializable interface, and ObjectOutputStream is used to write objects to a stream, while ObjectInputStream reads objects from a stream.

Example:

```
import java.io.*;
```

```java
public class User implements Serializable {
    private static final long serialVersionUID = 1L;
    private String name;
    private int age;

    public User(String name, int age) {
        this.name = name;
        this.age = age;
    }
}


// Serialization
try (ObjectOutputStream out = new
ObjectOutputStream(new
FileOutputStream("user.ser"))) {
    User user = new User("Alice", 30);
    out.writeObject(user);
}


// Deserialization
```

```java
try (ObjectInputStream in = new
ObjectInputStream(new FileInputStream("user.ser")))
{
    User user = (User) in.readObject();
    System.out.println(user.getName());
}
```

- **Limitations**: Java's built-in serialization can lead to large serialized data sizes, compatibility issues, and security vulnerabilities. It's often unsuitable for high-performance applications due to its verbosity and inefficiency.

2. Optimized Serialization with Protocol Buffers

Protocol Buffers (protobuf) is a language-neutral, platform-neutral, and efficient way to serialize structured data. Developed by Google, it's highly compact and suitable for high-performance applications, especially for inter-service communication in microservices architectures.

- **How It Works**: Developers define a .proto file to specify data structures, and the Protocol Buffer compiler generates Java classes that can serialize and deserialize these structures efficiently.

Example:

1. Define a .proto file:

proto

```proto
syntax = "proto3";

message User {
    string name = 1;
    int32 age = 2;
}
```

2. Compile the .proto file to generate Java classes.

3. Serialize and deserialize the data:

```java
User user =
User.newBuilder().setName("Alice").setAge(30).build();


// Serialization
byte[] data = user.toByteArray();


// Deserialization
User deserializedUser = User.parseFrom(data);
```

- **Advantages**: Protocol Buffers are compact, fast, and support backward compatibility, making them ideal for high-performance applications with frequent data exchanges between services.

3. Apache Avro for Schema Evolution

Apache Avro is another compact, fast, and flexible data serialization format commonly used with big data frameworks, such as Apache Hadoop and Kafka. Avro is designed for efficient serialization and schema evolution, allowing changes to data structures without breaking compatibility with previous versions.

- **How It Works**: Avro uses JSON to define schemas and stores data in a binary format, making it both human-readable (for schema) and highly compact (for data).

Example:

1. Define an Avro schema (in JSON format):

json

```
{
  "type": "record",
  "name": "User",
  "fields": [
    {"name": "name", "type": "string"},
```

```
    {"name": "age", "type": "int"}

  ]

}
```

2. Serialize and deserialize using the Avro library:

```
Schema schema = new Schema.Parser().parse(new File("user.avsc"));

GenericRecord user = new GenericData.Record(schema);

user.put("name", "Alice");

user.put("age", 30);


// Serialization

ByteArrayOutputStream out = new ByteArrayOutputStream();

DatumWriter<GenericRecord> writer = new GenericDatumWriter<>(schema);

Encoder encoder = EncoderFactory.get().binaryEncoder(out, null);

writer.write(user, encoder);

encoder.flush();

byte[] data = out.toByteArray();
```

// Deserialization

```
DatumReader<GenericRecord> reader = new
GenericDatumReader<>(schema);

Decoder decoder =
DecoderFactory.get().binaryDecoder(data, null);

GenericRecord deserializedUser = reader.read(null,
decoder);
```

- **Advantages**: Avro's schema evolution and compact format make it suitable for applications where data structures change frequently, such as APIs that require backward compatibility.

4. Custom Serialization

Custom serialization allows developers to control how objects are serialized and deserialized by implementing the Externalizable interface or defining writeObject and readObject methods.

- **How It Works**: Developers override writeObject and readObject to define custom serialization logic, making it possible to optimize data format and control object dependencies.

Example:

```java
public class User implements Serializable {

    private static final long serialVersionUID = 1L;

    private String name;

    private transient int age; // "transient" fields are not
serialized


    private void writeObject(ObjectOutputStream out)
throws IOException {

        out.defaultWriteObject();

        out.writeInt(age); // Custom serialization logic

    }


    private void readObject(ObjectInputStream in)
throws IOException, ClassNotFoundException {

        in.defaultReadObject();

        age = in.readInt(); // Custom deserialization logic

    }

}
```

Custom serialization can be useful when working with sensitive data, complex objects, or performance-critical applications, as it offers full control over the serialization process.

Using Protocol Buffers, Avro, and Custom Serialization in Practice

Protocol Buffers

Protocol Buffers are highly efficient for communication in distributed systems and are often used in microservices and API data transfer. They provide a compact and fast data format that supports schema evolution and allows backward compatibility.

Avro

Avro is optimized for big data applications, especially those requiring schema evolution and compatibility. It's frequently used with data pipelines, message brokers, and storage systems, making it ideal for high-throughput systems.

Custom Serialization

Custom serialization is particularly useful for complex Java objects that cannot be represented directly with standard serialization frameworks. This approach is essential for performance-critical systems that need tight control over data representation, often applied in game engines, scientific computations, or secure applications.

Case Study: Data Serialization for High-Performance APIs

Let's explore a case study where an API server handles high-frequency requests and must serialize data efficiently to meet performance and bandwidth requirements. This scenario will demonstrate how to select and implement the right serialization method for optimal performance.

Problem Statement

The API server receives thousands of requests per second, retrieving user data that needs to be serialized and sent back to the clients. The serialization format must be:

1. **Compact** to minimize bandwidth usage.

2. **Fast** to reduce serialization/deserialization time.

3. **Compatible** with future data structure changes.

Solution Using Protocol Buffers

Given the requirements, Protocol Buffers (protobuf) is a suitable choice due to its compact size, high performance, and schema evolution capabilities.
Here's how we'll set up the API server using Protocol Buffers for efficient data serialization.

1. **Define the Data Schema**

We define the data structure for the user information in a .proto file. This structure includes fields for id, name, email, and age.

proto

```
syntax = "proto3";

message User {
    int32 id = 1;
    string name = 2;
    string email = 3;
    int32 age = 4;
}
```

2. Compile the Protocol Buffer Definition

We compile the .proto file with the protobuf compiler to generate Java classes, enabling us to work with serialized and deserialized data easily.

Command to Compile:

bash

```
protoc --java_out=. user.proto
```

3. Implement Serialization and Deserialization in the API Server

Serialization: Convert the user data to a Protocol Buffers binary format when sending it to the client.

```
public byte[] serializeUser(User user) {

    return user.toByteArray();

}
```

Deserialization: Convert the Protocol Buffers binary format back into a User object when receiving data from the client or another service.

```
public User deserializeUser(byte[] data) throws
InvalidProtocolBufferException {

    return User.parseFrom(data);

}
```

4. Optimize Data Transmission with Protocol Buffers

Protocol Buffers produce a binary format that is much smaller than JSON or XML, reducing bandwidth usage and improving the response time for high-frequency API requests.

5. Testing and Performance Benchmarking

By testing the API's response times and network usage, we observe significant improvements compared to traditional JSON serialization. Here's a summary of performance gains:

- **Reduced Bandwidth**: Protocol Buffers reduce the size of data packets by 30–60% compared to JSON.

- **Faster Serialization/Deserialization**: The binary format of Protocol Buffers processes data faster than JSON parsing, decreasing CPU usage.

6. **Implementing Backward Compatibility with Schema Evolution**

Protocol Buffers allow us to add new fields in the .proto file without breaking older versions. By setting default values, we ensure that older clients can still read the serialized data even when new fields are added.

Updated .proto File with New Field:

proto

```
syntax = "proto3";


message User {
    int32 id = 1;
```

```
    string name = 2;

    string email = 3;

    int32 age = 4;

    string phone = 5; // New field for backward
compatibility

}
```

Conclusion

Serialization and deserialization are fundamental to building efficient distributed applications, especially in systems that need high-performance data exchange. In this chapter, we covered Java's built-in serialization, Protocol Buffers, Apache Avro, and custom serialization techniques, exploring their strengths and trade-offs for different use cases.

Through the case study on a high-performance API, we demonstrated how Protocol Buffers can optimize data transfer by minimizing bandwidth usage and processing time, making it ideal for high-throughput applications. By mastering these serialization techniques, Java developers can design applications that deliver efficient, reliable, and scalable data transfer across distributed systems.

Chapter 13: Multi-Platform Java Development

Java's "write once, run anywhere" philosophy makes it an ideal choice for developing applications across multiple platforms, including desktop, web, and mobile. With a unified codebase and cross-platform tools, developers can reach a broader audience and reduce development time and costs. In this chapter, we'll explore Java's capabilities for multi-platform development, discuss tools like JavaFX, Spring MVC, and Android SDK, and conclude with a practical example of building a cross-platform application for both mobile and desktop environments.

Developing Java Applications Across Desktop, Web, and Mobile Platforms

Java's versatility enables developers to build applications for a variety of platforms, each with its own set of frameworks, tools, and design principles. Here's an overview of Java's role in desktop, web, and mobile development.

1. Desktop Development with Java

Java has long been a popular choice for desktop applications, offering frameworks like **Swing** and **JavaFX** for building graphical user interfaces (GUIs). Desktop applications provide a rich, responsive interface for users who need software installed directly on their machines.

- **Swing**: Introduced in Java 1.2, Swing provides a set of components for building GUI applications. While Swing remains widely used, it has limitations in terms of modern UI design and flexibility.

- **JavaFX**: JavaFX, introduced in Java 8, is a more modern framework that supports advanced graphics, animations, and web integration. JavaFX is intended to replace Swing and provides better support for cross-platform development, making it the preferred choice for new desktop applications.

Example of JavaFX Application Setup:

```
import javafx.application.Application;
import javafx.scene.Scene;
```

```java
import javafx.scene.control.Label;
import javafx.stage.Stage;

public class DesktopApp extends Application {
    @Override
    public void start(Stage primaryStage) {
        Label label = new Label("Hello, JavaFX!");
        Scene scene = new Scene(label, 400, 200);
        primaryStage.setScene(scene);
        primaryStage.setTitle("JavaFX Desktop App");
        primaryStage.show();
    }

    public static void main(String[] args) {
        launch(args);
    }
}
```

This simple example shows how to create a JavaFX application with a single label displayed on a desktop window. JavaFX supports a range of features like animations, media playback, and custom controls, making it ideal for modern desktop applications.

2. Web Development with Java

Java is a powerful platform for web development, offering frameworks that support both server-side processing and client-server communication. **Spring MVC** and **JavaServer Faces (JSF)** are two of the most popular Java-based frameworks for building web applications.

- **Spring MVC**: Part of the Spring Framework, Spring MVC is a Model-View-Controller framework that simplifies building scalable, robust web applications. It is widely used in enterprise applications due to its flexibility and extensive ecosystem.

- **JavaServer Faces (JSF)**: JSF is a component-based framework for creating server-side UI components. While JSF is suitable for developing Java EE applications, it is less commonly used in modern Java web development due to its steep learning curve and limited flexibility compared to Spring MVC.

Example of a Basic Spring MVC Controller:

```
import org.springframework.stereotype.Controller;

import org.springframework.web.bind.annotation.GetMapping;
```

```java
import
org.springframework.web.bind.annotation.ResponseBo
dy;

@Controller
public class WebController {

    @GetMapping("/greet")
    @ResponseBody
    public String greet() {
        return "Hello, Spring MVC!";
    }
}
```

In this example, the WebController class defines a single route (/greet) that returns a greeting message. Spring MVC offers extensive features for handling HTTP requests, managing templates, and interfacing with databases, making it an ideal choice for building complex, scalable web applications.

3. Mobile Development with Java

Java is also a primary language for Android development, and the **Android SDK** provides all the necessary tools for creating native mobile applications. With the popularity of Android, Java developers can reach millions of mobile users by leveraging the Android SDK.

- **Android SDK**: The Android SDK provides libraries, tools, and APIs for building Android applications. Although Kotlin has become the preferred language for Android development, Java remains widely used and fully supported on the platform.

Example of an Android Activity:

java

```
import android.os.Bundle;

import android.widget.TextView;

import androidx.appcompat.app.AppCompatActivity;


public class MainActivity extends AppCompatActivity
{
    @Override
    protected void onCreate(Bundle savedInstanceState)
{
        super.onCreate(savedInstanceState);


        TextView textView = new TextView(this);
```

```
        textView.setText("Hello, Android!");

        setContentView(textView);

    }

}
```

In this example, we create a simple Android activity that displays a greeting message on the screen. Android provides a rich API for handling UI, sensors, notifications, and background tasks, allowing developers to build fully-featured mobile applications.

Tools for Cross-Platform Compatibility

Developing Java applications for multiple platforms can be streamlined using specific tools and frameworks that support cross-platform compatibility, enabling a unified codebase that runs on desktop, web, and mobile platforms.

1. JavaFX for Desktop and Web

JavaFX is primarily a desktop framework, but it also supports integration with HTML and JavaScript, allowing it to be embedded in web applications. JavaFX applications can run on Windows, macOS, and

Linux, making it a powerful tool for desktop development.

- **WebView**: JavaFX's WebView component enables embedding web content directly within a desktop application, facilitating hybrid applications.

- **JPro**: JPro is a JavaFX library that enables JavaFX applications to run directly in the browser, making it possible to deploy JavaFX applications as web applications.

2. Spring Boot and Spring MVC for REST APIs

Spring Boot simplifies building REST APIs that can be consumed by desktop, web, and mobile clients. A REST API provides a central backend that different platforms can interact with, creating a consistent data model and business logic layer across platforms.

- **REST Controllers**: Spring MVC supports creating RESTful endpoints that can be accessed from any platform, providing flexibility and compatibility across desktop, mobile, and web.

- **Spring Security**: Allows secure access to the API, handling authentication and authorization, which is essential for cross-platform applications.

3. Android SDK for Mobile Development

The Android SDK allows Java applications to run natively on mobile devices, providing access to device-specific features like GPS, camera, and notifications. It also supports integration with web services and REST APIs, enabling mobile clients to interact with backends developed in Java.

- **Retrofit**: A popular library for making HTTP requests in Android applications, which integrates seamlessly with Spring Boot APIs, facilitating consistent data sharing across mobile and web platforms.

Example: Building a Cross-Platform Mobile and Desktop Application

Let's create a cross-platform application that runs on both desktop and mobile. The application will display a list of user messages, retrieve them from a shared REST API, and allow users to view message details.

1. Setting Up the Spring Boot Backend

We start by building a Spring Boot REST API to handle message retrieval. This API will serve as the central data source for both the desktop and mobile applications.

API Controller for Message Retrieval:

```java
import org.springframework.web.bind.annotation.*;

import java.util.Arrays;
import java.util.List;

@RestController
@RequestMapping("/api/messages")
public class MessageController {

    @GetMapping
    public List<Message> getMessages() {
        return Arrays.asList(
            new Message(1, "Hello from Spring Boot!"),
            new Message(2, "Cross-platform Java
applications are amazing!")
        );
    }
}

class Message {
    private int id;
```

```java
    private String content;

    public Message(int id, String content) {
        this.id = id;
        this.content = content;
    }

    public int getId() { return id; }
    public String getContent() { return content; }
}
```

The MessageController returns a list of sample messages as JSON. This REST endpoint will be accessed by both the desktop and mobile applications.

2. Building the Desktop Application with JavaFX

The desktop application, built with JavaFX, fetches messages from the REST API and displays them in a list. Users can click a message to view its details.

JavaFX Application Code:

```java
import javafx.application.Application;
import javafx.scene.Scene;
import javafx.scene.control.*;
```

```java
import javafx.stage.Stage;

import javafx.scene.layout.VBox;

import java.io.BufferedReader;

import java.io.InputStreamReader;

import java.net.HttpURLConnection;

import java.net.URL;

import org.json.JSONArray;

import org.json.JSONObject;


public class DesktopApp extends Application {
    @Override
    public void start(Stage primaryStage) {
        ListView<String> listView = new ListView<>();
        listView.setPrefSize(400, 200);


        try {
            JSONArray messages = fetchMessages();
            for (int i = 0; i < messages.length(); i++) {
                JSONObject message =
messages.getJSONObject(i);
```

```java
listView.getItems().add(message.getString("content"));
        }
    } catch (Exception e) {
        e.printStackTrace();
    }

    VBox layout = new VBox(listView);
    Scene scene = new Scene(layout, 400, 200);
    primaryStage.setScene(scene);
    primaryStage.setTitle("JavaFX Desktop App");
    primaryStage.show();
}


private JSONArray fetchMessages() throws Exception {
    URL url = new URL("http://localhost:8080/api/messages");
    HttpURLConnection conn = (HttpURLConnection) url.openConnection();
    conn.setRequestMethod("GET");
```

```java
        BufferedReader in = new BufferedReader(new
InputStreamReader(conn.getInputStream()));

        StringBuilder response = new StringBuilder();

        String line;

        while ((line = in.readLine()) != null) {

            response.append(line);

        }

        in.close();


        return new JSONArray(response.toString());

    }


    public static void main(String[] args) {

        launch(args);

    }

}
```

This JavaFX application retrieves messages from the API and displays them in a ListView. The fetchMessages method sends an HTTP GET request to the Spring Boot API to retrieve message data.

3. Developing the Mobile Application with Android SDK

The mobile application will retrieve messages from the same API, display them in a list, and allow users to click on a message to view details.

Android MainActivity Code:

```
import android.os.Bundle;

import android.widget.ArrayAdapter;

import android.widget.ListView;

import androidx.appcompat.app.AppCompatActivity;

import org.json.JSONArray;

import org.json.JSONObject;

import java.io.BufferedReader;

import java.io.InputStreamReader;

import java.net.HttpURLConnection;

import java.net.URL;

import java.util.ArrayList;


public class MainActivity extends AppCompatActivity
{
    private ListView listView;
```

```java
    private ArrayList<String> messages;

    @Override
    protected void onCreate(Bundle savedInstanceState)
{

        super.onCreate(savedInstanceState);
        listView = new ListView(this);
        setContentView(listView);


        messages = new ArrayList<>();
        new Thread(this::fetchMessages).start();
    }


    private void fetchMessages() {
        try {
            URL url = new
URL("http://localhost:8080/api/messages");

            HttpURLConnection conn =
(HttpURLConnection) url.openConnection();

            conn.setRequestMethod("GET");
```

```java
        BufferedReader in = new BufferedReader(new
InputStreamReader(conn.getInputStream()));

        StringBuilder response = new StringBuilder();

        String line;

        while ((line = in.readLine()) != null) {

            response.append(line);

        }

        in.close();


        JSONArray messagesArray = new
JSONArray(response.toString());

        for (int i = 0; i < messagesArray.length(); i++)
{

        JSONObject message =
messagesArray.getJSONObject(i);

            messages.add(message.getString("content"));

        }


        runOnUiThread(() -> {

            ArrayAdapter<String> adapter = new
ArrayAdapter<>(this,
android.R.layout.simple_list_item_1, messages);

            listView.setAdapter(adapter);
```

```
        });

    } catch (Exception e) {

        e.printStackTrace();

    }

  }

}
```

The Android app's fetchMessages method retrieves data from the same Spring Boot API. An ArrayAdapter displays the messages in a ListView, giving users a consistent experience across desktop and mobile.

Conclusion

Java provides a powerful and versatile platform for developing applications across multiple platforms, including desktop, web, and mobile. In this chapter, we explored Java's capabilities for cross-platform development using JavaFX, Spring MVC, and Android SDK, and demonstrated how to build a unified backend with Spring Boot for cross-platform compatibility.

The example of a message-displaying application highlights how a single REST API can serve as the foundation for both desktop and mobile applications, allowing for a consistent user experience. By leveraging Java's cross-platform tools, developers can efficiently create applications that reach a broad audience, from desktop users to mobile customers.

Chapter 14: Java for Big Data and Machine Learning

Java's robustness, scalability, and extensive ecosystem make it an excellent choice for big data and machine learning applications. With Java-based big data tools like Apache Spark and Hadoop, and machine learning libraries like Deep Java Library (DJL) and Apache Mahout, developers can build powerful, data-driven applications directly in Java. This chapter covers how to integrate Java with big data tools, build and deploy machine learning models, and presents a practical case study on developing a recommendation system for an e-commerce platform.

Integrating Java with Big Data Tools

Big data applications require tools that can handle large volumes of data, process it efficiently, and scale as needed. Java-based big data tools like Apache Hadoop and Apache Spark are widely used in industry due to their performance and scalability. Let's explore how Java integrates with these tools to process and analyze data.

1. Apache Hadoop

Apache Hadoop is a framework for distributed storage and processing of large datasets across clusters of computers. It uses a distributed file system (HDFS) and provides tools for batch processing and managing large-scale data.

- **Hadoop Distributed File System (HDFS)**: HDFS stores large datasets across multiple nodes, ensuring high availability and fault tolerance.

- **MapReduce**: A processing model that distributes tasks across multiple nodes, allowing data processing to scale efficiently.

Example of a Simple Hadoop MapReduce Job:

A MapReduce job consists of two main components: a Mapper, which processes each data element, and a Reducer, which aggregates results.

1. **Mapper Class**:

```
import org.apache.hadoop.io.IntWritable;

import org.apache.hadoop.io.Text;

import org.apache.hadoop.mapreduce.Mapper;


public class WordCountMapper extends
Mapper<Object, Text, Text, IntWritable> {
```

```java
    private final static IntWritable one = new
IntWritable(1);

    private Text word = new Text();


    public void map(Object key, Text value, Context
context) {

        String[] words = value.toString().split("\\s+");

        for (String str : words) {

            word.set(str);

            context.write(word, one);

        }

    }

}
```

2. **Reducer Class**:

```java
import org.apache.hadoop.io.IntWritable;

import org.apache.hadoop.io.Text;

import org.apache.hadoop.mapreduce.Reducer;


public class WordCountReducer extends
Reducer<Text, IntWritable, Text, IntWritable> {
```

```
public void reduce(Text key, Iterable<IntWritable>
values, Context context) {

    int sum = 0;

    for (IntWritable val : values) {

        sum += val.get();

    }

    context.write(key, new IntWritable(sum));

  }

}
```

This example demonstrates a basic word count program, where the Mapper counts occurrences of each word and the Reducer sums these counts. Although Hadoop is well-suited for batch processing, its limitations in real-time analytics led to the development of Apache Spark.

2. Apache Spark

Apache Spark is a fast, in-memory big data processing engine that supports both batch and real-time data processing. It's widely used in data analytics and machine learning applications due to its speed and flexibility.

- **Resilient Distributed Dataset (RDD)**: Spark's core data structure, RDDs allow parallel processing across clusters and provide fault tolerance.

- **DataFrame and Spark SQL**: Higher-level abstractions that simplify working with structured data, such as SQL tables and DataFrames.

Example of a Simple Spark Application in Java:

```java
import org.apache.spark.api.java.JavaRDD;

import org.apache.spark.api.java.JavaSparkContext;

import org.apache.spark.SparkConf;


public class SparkWordCount {
    public static void main(String[] args) {

        SparkConf conf = new SparkConf().setAppName("Spark Word Count").setMaster("local[*]");

        JavaSparkContext sc = new JavaSparkContext(conf);


        JavaRDD<String> lines = sc.textFile("input.txt");

        JavaRDD<String> words = lines.flatMap(line -> Arrays.asList(line.split(" ")).iterator());

        JavaPairRDD<String, Integer> wordCounts = words.mapToPair(word -> new Tuple2<>(word, 1))
```

```
.reduceByKey(Integer::sum);


    wordCounts.foreach(data ->
System.out.println(data._1() + ": " + data._2()));

    sc.close();

  }

}
```

This example reads data from a text file, splits it into words, and counts occurrences using Spark's RDD and functional transformations. Spark's in-memory processing provides a significant speed advantage over Hadoop, especially for iterative processing and machine learning tasks.

Building and Deploying Machine Learning Models in Java Applications

With the rise of machine learning, Java has adapted to support model training and deployment through various libraries and frameworks, making it possible to build intelligent applications that can classify, predict, and recommend in real time.

1. Machine Learning Libraries in Java

Java offers several libraries for building machine learning models, with options suited to different needs.

- **Apache Mahout**: A scalable machine learning library that works with Hadoop for distributed processing. It supports clustering, classification, and recommendation algorithms, making it ideal for big data applications.

- **Deep Java Library (DJL)**: An open-source library for training and deploying deep learning models in Java, built on popular frameworks like TensorFlow, PyTorch, and MXNet.

2. Building a Machine Learning Model with DJL

DJL simplifies integrating deep learning models into Java applications. It provides APIs for building, training, and deploying models, with pre-trained models available for common tasks.

Example of a Simple Image Classification Model Using DJL:

```
import ai.djl.Model;
import ai.djl.ModelException;
```

```java
import ai.djl.inference.Predictor;

import ai.djl.modality.Classifications;

import ai.djl.modality.cv.Image;

import ai.djl.modality.cv.ImageFactory;

import ai.djl.translate.TranslateException;


public class ImageClassifier {
    public static void main(String[] args) throws
ModelException, TranslateException {
        String modelPath = "path/to/model.zip";

        Image img =
ImageFactory.getInstance().fromFile(Paths.get("path/to/image.jpg"));


        try (Model model =
Model.newInstance(modelPath);

            Predictor<Image, Classifications> predictor =
model.newPredictor()) {

            Classifications result = predictor.predict(img);

            System.out.println(result);
        }
    }
```

```
}
```

In this example, DJL loads a pre-trained model and uses it to classify an input image. This setup allows Java applications to perform deep learning inference tasks with minimal code.

3. Deploying Machine Learning Models with Java

Java applications can deploy machine learning models in several ways, including:

- **Embedded Deployment**: Using a machine learning library like DJL to embed models directly into the Java application.

- **REST API Deployment**: Exposing the model as a REST API, often using Spring Boot, to serve predictions to other applications.

- **Apache Kafka for Streaming**: Integrating with Apache Kafka to process real-time data streams, allowing models to make predictions on data as it arrives.

Example of a REST API Model Deployment:

```
import org.springframework.web.bind.annotation.*;

import ai.djl.Model;

import ai.djl.inference.Predictor;

import ai.djl.modality.Classifications;
```

```java
import ai.djl.modality.Classifications.Classification;
import ai.djl.modality.nlp.NlpProcess;
import ai.djl.translate.TranslateException;


@RestController
@RequestMapping("/api/predict")
public class PredictionController {

    private Model model;
    private Predictor<NlpProcess, Classifications> predictor;

    public PredictionController() throws ModelException {
        model = Model.newInstance("path/to/model");
        predictor = model.newPredictor();
    }


    @PostMapping
    public String predict(@RequestBody String input) throws TranslateException {
```

```
Classifications result = predictor.predict(new
NlpProcess(input));

Classification classification = result.best();

return classification.getClassName() + ": " +
classification.getProbability();

    }

}
```

This REST API example exposes the model as an endpoint, allowing other applications to send input data and receive predictions.

Case Study: Recommendation System for an E-Commerce Platform

Let's apply these principles in a practical case study of building a recommendation system for an e-commerce platform. This system will analyze user behavior and provide product recommendations.

Problem Statement

Our e-commerce platform needs a recommendation system to suggest products based on users' browsing and purchasing histories. The system should be:

1. **Scalable** to handle a large number of users and products.

2. **Efficient** in generating recommendations in real time.

3. **Customizable** to support different recommendation algorithms.

Solution Using Apache Spark and Apache Mahout

We'll use Apache Spark for data processing and Apache Mahout to build a collaborative filtering model, a common algorithm for recommendation systems.

1. Data Preprocessing with Apache Spark

First, we use Spark to process data on user interactions, such as product views and purchases, which are stored in a distributed database. Spark transforms this data into a matrix format suitable for input to the Mahout recommendation model.

Example of Data Preprocessing with Spark:

```
JavaRDD<String> rawData =
sc.textFile("user_interactions.csv");

JavaRDD<Rating> ratings = rawData.map(line -> {

    String[] fields = line.split(",");
```

```
    return new Rating(Integer.parseInt(fields[0]),
Integer.parseInt(fields[1]),
Double.parseDouble(fields[2]));

});
```

This example reads user interactions from a CSV file and converts each interaction into a Rating object, which stores user ID, product ID, and rating.

2. Building the Recommendation Model with Apache Mahout

We use Mahout's collaborative filtering algorithm to create a recommendation model that identifies relationships between users and products.

Example of Mahout Collaborative Filtering Model:

```
DataModel model = new FileDataModel(new
File("user_interactions.csv"));

UserSimilarity similarity = new
PearsonCorrelationSimilarity(model);

UserBasedRecommender recommender = new
GenericUserBasedRecommender(model, similarity,
new NearestNUserNeighborhood(10, similarity,
model));


List<RecommendedItem> recommendations =
recommender.recommend(userId, 5);
```

```
for (RecommendedItem recommendation :
recommendations) {

    System.out.println("Product ID: " +
recommendation.getItemID() + " Score: " +
recommendation.getValue());

}
```

This example uses Mahout's GenericUserBasedRecommender to recommend products for a given user based on similarity to other users.

3. **Deploying the Recommendation System**

We deploy the recommendation system using a REST API with Spring Boot, allowing the application to serve recommendations to the e-commerce platform.

Spring Boot REST API for Recommendations:

```
@RestController

@RequestMapping("/api/recommend")

public class RecommendationController {

    @GetMapping("/{userId}")

    public List<String>
recommendProducts(@PathVariable int userId) {

        return
recommendationService.getRecommendations(userId);
```

```
  }
}
```

This API endpoint allows the client to request product recommendations for a user by ID, which the backend processes using the Mahout model.

Conclusion

Java's integration with big data tools and machine learning frameworks enables developers to build scalable, data-driven applications for various use cases, from data processing to recommendation systems. In this chapter, we explored how to use Java with big data tools like Apache Spark and Hadoop, build machine learning models with DJL and Mahout, and deploy models in real-time environments.

Through the case study on a recommendation system for an e-commerce platform, we demonstrated how Java's capabilities in big data and machine learning can be applied to solve complex business problems, offering users personalized, data-driven experiences. Mastering these tools and techniques empowers Java developers to build intelligent applications that scale with demand and leverage data insights for real-world impact.

Part 4

Building and Maintaining Resilient Java Systems

Chapter 15: Dependency Injection and Inversion of Control

Dependency Injection (DI) and Inversion of Control (IoC) are essential principles in modern software design, enabling modularity, scalability, and ease of testing. By decoupling components, DI and IoC allow systems to grow and change without significant refactoring, making them ideal for enterprise-scale applications. This chapter explores the core principles of dependency injection, the benefits for building scalable systems, how to use Spring's IoC container to manage dependencies, and an example of a modular architecture in an enterprise Java application.

Dependency Injection Principles and Benefits for Scalable Systems

In traditional programming, classes often instantiate their dependencies directly, leading to tight coupling between components. Tight coupling makes applications hard to test, scale, and maintain because changes in one component can impact others, creating a cascade of required modifications. Dependency Injection (DI) and Inversion of Control (IoC) address these issues by allowing dependencies to be managed externally, making classes more modular and easier to test.

1. Understanding Dependency Injection

Dependency Injection is a design pattern that provides an object's dependencies from an external source rather than having the object create its own dependencies. DI allows developers to inject (provide) dependencies into a class, rather than having the class construct them.

- **Dependencies**: Components or services that a class requires to perform its operations.

- **Injection**: Providing dependencies from the outside, usually via constructors, setters, or interface methods.

Example of Dependency Injection:

Without DI:

```
public class OrderService {

    private PaymentService paymentService = new PaymentService();

    private InventoryService inventoryService = new InventoryService();
```

```java
    public void placeOrder(Order order) {

        paymentService.processPayment(order.getAmount());

        inventoryService.updateInventory(order.getProductId(
));;
    }
}
```

With DI:

```java
public class OrderService {
    private final PaymentService paymentService;
    private final InventoryService inventoryService;

    public OrderService(PaymentService
paymentService, InventoryService inventoryService) {
        this.paymentService = paymentService;
        this.inventoryService = inventoryService;
    }

    public void placeOrder(Order order) {
```

```
paymentService.processPayment(order.getAmount());

inventoryService.updateInventory(order.getProductId(
));
    }
}
```

In this example, OrderService no longer creates
instances of PaymentService and InventoryService.
Instead, they are provided from outside, promoting
flexibility and testability.

2. Types of Dependency Injection

There are three main types of dependency injection:

- **Constructor Injection**: Dependencies are
  provided through the class constructor, making
  them immutable after instantiation.

- **Setter Injection**: Dependencies are injected
  using setter methods, allowing optional
  dependencies and making it possible to change
  dependencies at runtime.

- **Interface Injection**: Dependencies are injected
  by implementing a specific interface, though
  this is less common in Java.

Example of Setter Injection:

```
public class OrderService {

    private PaymentService paymentService;


    public void setPaymentService(PaymentService
    paymentService) {

        this.paymentService = paymentService;

    }


    public void placeOrder(Order order) {

paymentService.processPayment(order.getAmount());

    }

}
```

3. Benefits of Dependency Injection for Scalable Systems

- **Modularity**: By decoupling components, DI allows each class to focus on a single responsibility, making it easier to understand, extend, and maintain.

- **Testability**: DI enables testing by injecting mock dependencies, making it easier to isolate and verify each component's behavior.

- **Scalability**: DI supports modularity and loose coupling, allowing systems to scale by adding new modules and components without changing existing ones.

- **Reusability**: Components with injected dependencies are more flexible and reusable in other contexts because they're not tightly coupled with specific implementations.

Dependency Injection plays a critical role in building scalable systems by promoting a clean, modular structure that grows and adapts to changing requirements.

Using Spring's IoC Container for Creating Modular Applications

The Spring Framework provides a powerful IoC container that manages the lifecycle and dependencies of Java objects, enabling efficient dependency injection for scalable, enterprise-level applications. Spring's IoC container supports DI through configuration metadata, either using XML, Java annotations, or Java-based configuration.

1. Understanding Spring's IoC Container

Spring's IoC container is responsible for instantiating, configuring, and managing objects and their dependencies. It allows developers to define beans, which represent the components of an application, and configure dependencies between them.

- **Beans**: Spring beans are objects managed by the Spring IoC container. A bean can be any POJO (Plain Old Java Object) with optional configuration metadata specifying how it should be created and managed.

- **ApplicationContext**: The ApplicationContext is the central interface to Spring's IoC container, providing bean lifecycle management, dependency injection, and resource management.

2. Configuring Beans in Spring

Beans in Spring can be configured in multiple ways, including:

- **XML Configuration**: Although less common now, XML configuration allows developers to define beans and their dependencies in an XML file.

- **Annotations**: Annotations like @Component, @Service, and @Autowired allow for simplified configuration directly in the code.

- **Java-Based Configuration**: Using @Configuration classes, Java-based configuration provides a more type-safe and IDE-friendly approach to configuring beans.

Example of Java-Based Configuration:

```java
import org.springframework.context.annotation.Bean;
import org.springframework.context.annotation.Configuration;

@Configuration
public class AppConfig {

    @Bean
    public PaymentService paymentService() {
        return new PaymentService();
    }

    @Bean
    public OrderService orderService() {
        return new OrderService(paymentService(),
inventoryService());
    }

    @Bean
    public InventoryService inventoryService() {
```

```
        return new InventoryService();

    }

}
```

In this example, the AppConfig class defines three beans: PaymentService, OrderService, and InventoryService. The orderService bean depends on the other two, and Spring automatically resolves these dependencies.

3. Dependency Injection with Spring Annotations

Spring offers annotations to simplify dependency injection, making it easier to define and wire beans within an application. Common annotations include:

- **@Autowired**: Injects dependencies automatically, reducing boilerplate code.

- **@Component, @Service, @Repository**: Mark classes as Spring-managed beans, allowing them to be detected and instantiated automatically.

Example Using Annotations:

```
import
org.springframework.beans.factory.annotation.Autowir
ed;

import org.springframework.stereotype.Service;
```

```java
@Service
public class OrderService {
    private final PaymentService paymentService;
    private final InventoryService inventoryService;

    @Autowired
    public OrderService(PaymentService paymentService, InventoryService inventoryService) {
        this.paymentService = paymentService;
        this.inventoryService = inventoryService;
    }

    public void placeOrder(Order order) {

        paymentService.processPayment(order.getAmount());

        inventoryService.updateInventory(order.getProductId());
    }
}
```

With @Autowired, Spring automatically injects the PaymentService and InventoryService dependencies into OrderService.

Example: Modular Architecture for an Enterprise Java Application

Let's build a modular enterprise Java application using Spring's IoC container and dependency injection. In this example, we'll create a simple e-commerce application with separate modules for processing orders, managing inventory, and handling payments.

Problem Statement

The e-commerce application should have a modular architecture that enables easy maintenance, testing, and scalability. It should include:

1. An OrderService to process orders.

2. An InventoryService to manage inventory levels.

3. A PaymentService to handle payments.

Each module should be independent, allowing for future changes and enhancements without affecting other modules.

Solution Design Using Dependency Injection and Spring's IoC Container

1. **Defining Service Interfaces**

To create a modular architecture, we define service interfaces for each module. This allows us to separate implementation from the interface, making it easy to swap implementations if needed.

```java
public interface PaymentService {

    void processPayment(double amount);

}


public interface InventoryService {

    void updateInventory(String productId);

}


public interface OrderService {

    void placeOrder(Order order);

}
```

2. Implementing Service Classes

We implement these interfaces in concrete classes. Each class focuses on a single responsibility, keeping the application modular and maintainable.

```java
import org.springframework.stereotype.Service;
```

```java
@Service

public class PaymentServiceImpl implements
PaymentService {

    @Override

    public void processPayment(double amount) {

        System.out.println("Processing payment of $" +
amount);

    }

}


@Service

public class InventoryServiceImpl implements
InventoryService {

    @Override

    public void updateInventory(String productId) {

        System.out.println("Updating inventory for
product ID: " + productId);

    }

}


@Service
```

```java
public class OrderServiceImpl implements
OrderService {

    private final PaymentService paymentService;

    private final InventoryService inventoryService;


    public OrderServiceImpl(PaymentService
paymentService, InventoryService inventoryService) {

        this.paymentService = paymentService;

        this.inventoryService = inventoryService;

    }


    @Override
    public void placeOrder(Order order) {

paymentService.processPayment(order.getAmount());

inventoryService.updateInventory(order.getProductId(
));
        System.out.println("Order placed successfully for
product ID: " + order.getProductId());

    }
}
```

3. Configuring the Application with Spring Boot

Using Spring Boot, we can configure the application as a standalone service with minimal setup. Spring Boot's autoconfiguration will automatically detect and wire the beans defined by @Service annotations.

Spring Boot Main Application:

```
import org.springframework.boot.SpringApplication;

import org.springframework.boot.autoconfigure.SpringBootApplication;


@SpringBootApplication

public class ECommerceApplication {

    public static void main(String[] args) {


SpringApplication.run(ECommerceApplication.class, args);

    }

}
```

4. Creating an API Layer for Order Placement

We expose the OrderService functionality through a REST API, allowing clients to place orders. This API serves as the entry point for interacting with the application.

java

```java
import org.springframework.beans.factory.annotation.Autowired;
import org.springframework.web.bind.annotation.*;

@RestController
@RequestMapping("/api/orders")
public class OrderController {

    private final OrderService orderService;

    @Autowired
    public OrderController(OrderService orderService) {
        this.orderService = orderService;
    }

    @PostMapping
```

```
    public String placeOrder(@RequestBody Order
order) {

        orderService.placeOrder(order);

        return "Order placed successfully!";

    }

}
```

Here, the OrderController receives an HTTP POST
request and calls OrderService.placeOrder() to process
the order.

5. Testing and Running the Application

With Spring's IoC container managing dependencies,
we can now run and test the application. Spring Boot
handles the injection of PaymentService and
InventoryService into OrderService, providing a
modular and scalable setup.

6. Adding New Modules

With the IoC and DI setup, adding new services, like a
ShippingService or NotificationService, becomes
straightforward. Spring's IoC container will manage
the new dependencies, making it easy to integrate
additional modules without modifying existing code.

Conclusion

Dependency Injection and Inversion of Control are foundational principles for creating modular, scalable, and maintainable Java applications. In this chapter, we covered the benefits of DI, explored different types of injection, and showed how Spring's IoC container simplifies dependency management in enterprise applications.

The example of a modular e-commerce application demonstrates how DI and IoC support a clean, maintainable architecture that scales with new modules. By mastering DI and leveraging Spring's IoC container, Java developers can build flexible applications that adapt to evolving requirements, making DI a critical skill in enterprise software development.

Chapter 16:
Continuous Integration and Deployment (CI/CD)

In modern software development, **Continuous Integration (CI)** and **Continuous Deployment (CD)** are essential practices that help automate the building, testing, and deployment of applications. CI/CD pipelines increase productivity by catching issues early in the development cycle, ensuring consistency, and enabling rapid, reliable releases. This chapter explores the principles of CI/CD, how to set up pipelines using Jenkins, GitLab CI, and GitHub Actions, and concludes with a practical workflow for CI/CD in a high-availability microservices architecture.

Setting Up CI/CD Pipelines with Jenkins, GitLab CI, and GitHub Actions

CI/CD pipelines streamline the software delivery process by automating tasks such as code integration, testing, and deployment. Let's explore how to create CI/CD pipelines using three popular tools: **Jenkins**, **GitLab CI**, and **GitHub Actions**.

1. Jenkins for CI/CD

Jenkins is an open-source automation server that allows developers to build, test, and deploy applications. Known for its flexibility, Jenkins integrates with numerous plugins and supports a variety of programming languages and deployment platforms.

Setting Up a Jenkins Pipeline

1. **Install Jenkins**: Download and install Jenkins from the official website. Run it locally or on a server, ensuring it has access to your project's repository.

2. **Configure Jenkins Pipeline**: Create a new pipeline in Jenkins by navigating to **New Item** and selecting **Pipeline**.

3. **Write the Jenkinsfile**: Define your pipeline in a Jenkinsfile, which Jenkins uses to automate CI/CD tasks.

Example Jenkinsfile for a Java Application:

groovy

```
pipeline {
   agent any

   stages {
      stage('Build') {
         steps {
            sh 'mvn clean package'
         }
      }
      stage('Test') {
         steps {
            sh 'mvn test'
         }
      }
      stage('Deploy') {
         steps {
            sh 'scp target/myapp.jar
user@server:/path/to/deploy'

            sh 'ssh user@server "systemctl restart
myapp"'
         }
```

```
        }
    }
}
```

- **Build Stage**: Compiles the application.

- **Test Stage**: Runs unit tests to ensure code quality.

- **Deploy Stage**: Transfers the built application to the server and restarts it.

4. **Run the Pipeline**: Save the Jenkinsfile in your project's repository and trigger the pipeline manually or by configuring a webhook to start the process on each commit.

2. GitLab CI for CI/CD

GitLab CI is a built-in CI/CD tool in GitLab that allows you to define and run CI/CD pipelines using .gitlab-ci.yml. GitLab CI is tightly integrated with GitLab repositories, making it an excellent choice for teams using GitLab as their version control platform.

Setting Up a GitLab CI Pipeline

1. **Create .gitlab-ci.yml File**: Define the pipeline stages and tasks in a .gitlab-ci.yml file located in the root of your project repository.

Example .gitlab-ci.yml for a Java Application:

yaml

```yaml
stages:
  - build
  - test
  - deploy

build:
  stage: build
  script:
    - mvn clean package
  artifacts:
    paths:
      - target/*.jar

test:
  stage: test
  script:
    - mvn test

deploy:
  stage: deploy
```

script:

- scp target/myapp.jar user@server:/path/to/deploy

- ssh user@server "systemctl restart myapp"

only:

- main

2. **Pipeline Stages**:

   - **build**: Compiles the Java application and stores the .jar file as an artifact.

   - **test**: Runs automated tests to validate the application.

   - **deploy**: Deploys the application to a server when changes are merged to the main branch.

3. **Triggering the Pipeline**: Push changes to GitLab, and the pipeline automatically triggers based on the .gitlab-ci.yml configuration.

3. GitHub Actions for CI/CD

GitHub Actions is GitHub's native CI/CD tool, allowing you to define workflows using YAML files. With GitHub Actions, developers can automate build, test, and deploy steps directly in their GitHub repository.

Setting Up a GitHub Actions Workflow

1. **Create Workflow File**: Create a .github/workflows/ci.yml file in your repository to define the pipeline stages.

Example GitHub Actions Workflow for a Java Application:

yaml

```yaml
name: Java CI/CD Pipeline

on:
  push:
    branches:
      - main

jobs:
  build:
    runs-on: ubuntu-latest

    steps:
      - name: Checkout code
        uses: actions/checkout@v2
```

```yaml
    - name: Set up JDK
      uses: actions/setup-java@v2
      with:
        java-version: '11'

    - name: Build with Maven
      run: mvn clean package

    - name: Run tests
      run: mvn test

    - name: Deploy to server
      if: github.ref == 'refs/heads/main'
      env:
        SERVER_USER: ${{ secrets.SERVER_USER }}
        SERVER_HOST: ${{ secrets.SERVER_HOST }}
      run: |
        scp target/myapp.jar $SERVER_USER@$SERVER_HOST:/path/to/deploy
```

```
ssh $SERVER_USER@$SERVER_HOST
"systemctl restart myapp"
```

2. **Workflow Steps**:

   - **Build with Maven**: Compiles the Java
     application.

   - **Run tests**: Executes unit tests.

   - **Deploy to Server**: Deploys the
     application to a remote server only on
     changes to the main branch.

3. **Automating Deployment with Secrets**: Store
   sensitive information like server credentials as
   secrets in GitHub to secure your deployment
   process.

Automated Testing and Deployment for Scalable Applications

CI/CD pipelines automate the build and deployment
process, ensuring that only thoroughly tested code
reaches production. Here are key elements to consider
for robust automated testing and deployment.

1. Automated Testing Strategies

- **Unit Tests**: Tests individual components in isolation, verifying functionality at the smallest level. Tools: JUnit, TestNG.

- **Integration Tests**: Tests the interaction between components, such as API calls or database connections. Tools: Spring Test, REST-assured.

- **End-to-End (E2E) Tests**: Simulates real user interactions to ensure the entire application works as expected. Tools: Selenium, Cypress.

Example of a Unit Test with JUnit:

```java
import static org.junit.jupiter.api.Assertions.*;
import org.junit.jupiter.api.Test;

public class OrderServiceTest {

    @Test
    public void testPlaceOrder() {
        OrderService orderService = new OrderService(new PaymentService(), new InventoryService());
        Order order = new Order(1, "product123", 100);
        assertTrue(orderService.placeOrder(order));
```

```
    }
}
```

2. Automated Deployment

Automated deployment ensures consistent and reliable releases, minimizing manual intervention and reducing the risk of errors.

- **Canary Deployment**: Deploys new versions to a small subset of servers first, allowing monitoring before full release.

- **Blue-Green Deployment**: Maintains two identical environments; one serves production traffic (blue), while the other is prepared for the next release (green).

- **Rolling Deployment**: Updates a few servers at a time to avoid downtime, gradually rolling out the new version.

Practical Workflow: CI/CD for a High-Availability Microservices Setup

In a high-availability microservices architecture, multiple services work together to deliver functionality. Each service has its own CI/CD pipeline to ensure updates are independently deployed without downtime or disruption to other services.

Scenario Overview

An e-commerce application consists of three microservices:

1. **User Service**: Manages user accounts and authentication.

2. **Product Service**: Manages product information.

3. **Order Service**: Processes orders and payments.

Each service has its own repository, CI/CD pipeline, and deployment environment.

Step-by-Step CI/CD Workflow for Microservices

1. Define Individual Pipelines for Each Service

Each service has its own pipeline configuration. This example uses GitLab CI for simplicity, but similar setups can be achieved with Jenkins or GitHub Actions.

Example .gitlab-ci.yml for the User Service:

yaml

```
stages:
  - build
```

```
  - test
  - deploy

build:
  stage: build
  script:
    - mvn clean package
  artifacts:
    paths:
      - target/*.jar

test:
  stage: test
  script:
    - mvn test

deploy:
  stage: deploy
  script:
    - kubectl apply -f kubernetes/user-service.yaml
  only:
```

- main

- o **Build and Test Stages**: Run unit and integration tests for code quality.

- o **Deploy Stage**: Deploys the service to a Kubernetes cluster using kubectl, which is configured to deploy only from the main branch.

2. **Use Kubernetes for High-Availability Deployment**

Each service is deployed on a Kubernetes cluster, which provides automated scaling, load balancing, and self-healing capabilities.

Example Kubernetes Deployment YAML for User Service:

yaml

```
apiVersion: apps/v1
kind: Deployment
metadata:
  name: user-service
spec:
  replicas: 3
```

```
  selector:
    matchLabels:
      app: user-service
  template:
    metadata:
      labels:
        app: user-service
    spec:
      containers:
      - name: user-service
        image: myregistry/user-service:latest
        ports:
        - containerPort: 8080
```

This configuration specifies that three replicas of the user-service should be created, ensuring high availability and load balancing.

3. **Implement Canary Deployment with Kubernetes**

To avoid full-scale rollout issues, we configure a canary deployment to deploy new versions to a small percentage of users initially.

- o **Service Configuration for Canary**: Deploy the new version to a subset of replicas.

- o **Monitor the Canary**: Track the performance of the canary release using Kubernetes monitoring tools (e.g., Prometheus, Grafana). If stable, gradually increase traffic to the new version.

4. **Automate Testing at Multiple Levels**

Each microservice should have its own automated testing strategy:

- o **Unit and Integration Tests**: Run these in the CI pipeline.

- o **End-to-End Tests**: Perform comprehensive E2E tests on the staging environment before production deployment.

5. **Monitor and Rollback if Necessary**

Continuous deployment can introduce issues if a release fails. Set up monitoring and alerting to detect issues in real time and roll back the deployment automatically if necessary.

Conclusion

Continuous Integration and Deployment (CI/CD) pipelines are essential for modern software development, enabling developers to automate build, test, and deploy tasks. In this chapter, we explored CI/CD pipelines with Jenkins, GitLab CI, and GitHub Actions, highlighted the importance of automated testing and deployment, and walked through a practical CI/CD workflow for a high-availability microservices setup.

By integrating CI/CD practices, developers can maintain code quality, ensure reliability, and deliver updates faster. Mastering CI/CD tools and principles empowers teams to build and deploy applications with confidence and efficiency, essential for success in dynamic software environments.

Chapter 17: Testing and Debugging Strategies

Testing and debugging are essential components of software development, ensuring code reliability, quality, and resilience. Effective testing strategies catch issues early in the development cycle, saving time and reducing costs by preventing bugs from reaching production. In this chapter, we'll explore test-driven development (TDD) and behavior-driven development (BDD), advanced testing techniques using JUnit, Mockito, and integration testing, and conclude with a practical scenario focused on testing a complex distributed system.

Test-Driven Development (TDD) and Behavior-Driven Development (BDD)

Test-Driven Development (TDD) and **Behavior-Driven Development (BDD)** are popular methodologies that help developers create robust, maintainable code through systematic testing practices.

1. Test-Driven Development (TDD)

TDD is a software development approach where tests are written before the actual code. In TDD, developers follow a cycle of **writing a failing test, writing code to pass the test, and then refactoring** the code to improve quality. This ensures that each feature or functionality is verified immediately as it is implemented.

Benefits of TDD:

- **Code Quality**: Writing tests first encourages developers to write modular, loosely coupled code.

- **Early Bug Detection**: TDD helps catch bugs early in the development process.

- **Improved Confidence**: A robust suite of unit tests provides confidence in the codebase and facilitates safe refactoring.

Example TDD Cycle for a Calculator Method:

1. **Write a Failing Test**:

```
@Test
public void testAddition() {
    Calculator calc = new Calculator();
```

```
    assertEquals(5, calc.add(2, 3));

}
```

Since there is no add method in Calculator, this test will fail.

2. **Write Code to Pass the Test**:

```
public class Calculator {

    public int add(int a, int b) {

        return a + b;

    }

}
```

Now the test should pass as we've implemented the add method.

3. **Refactor**: Improve the code structure without changing its behavior. In this case, there might be no need to refactor, but as the code grows, TDD's refactoring step helps ensure maintainability.

2. Behavior-Driven Development (BDD)

BDD is an extension of TDD that emphasizes **collaboration between developers, testers, and non-technical stakeholders**. BDD focuses on describing the behavior of an application in terms that all stakeholders can understand, often using natural language.

In Java, BDD can be implemented with frameworks like **Cucumber**, where specifications are written in Gherkin syntax to define behaviors and outcomes in plain language.

Example BDD Scenario with Cucumber:

1. **Feature File** (Calculator.feature):

gherkin

Feature: Calculator addition

  Scenario: Adding two numbers

    Given I have entered 2 into the calculator

    And I have entered 3 into the calculator

    When I press add

    Then the result should be 5

2. **Step Definitions**:

```
import io.cucumber.java.en.*;

public class CalculatorSteps {
    private Calculator calculator;
```

```java
    private int result;

    @Given("I have entered {int} into the calculator")
    public void enterNumber(int number) {
        calculator.enter(number);
    }

    @When("I press add")
    public void pressAdd() {
        result = calculator.add();
    }

    @Then("the result should be {int}")
    public void verifyResult(int expected) {
        assertEquals(expected, result);
    }
}
```

By using BDD, developers can create a shared understanding of application requirements, bridging the gap between business and technical teams.

Advanced Testing Techniques with JUnit, Mockito, and Integration Testing

Testing frameworks like **JUnit** and **Mockito** are central to modern Java testing practices. Combined with integration testing strategies, they enable developers to verify application functionality at various levels.

1. JUnit for Unit Testing

JUnit is the standard framework for unit testing in Java, allowing developers to create automated tests and organize them into suites.

- **Annotations**: JUnit provides annotations like @Test, @BeforeEach, and @AfterEach to manage test setup and teardown.

- **Assertions**: JUnit offers a range of assertions (assertEquals, assertTrue, assertNotNull, etc.) to verify expected outcomes.

Example of a JUnit Test:

import static org.junit.jupiter.api.Assertions.*;

import org.junit.jupiter.api.BeforeEach;

```java
import org.junit.jupiter.api.Test;

public class CalculatorTest {
    private Calculator calculator;

    @BeforeEach
    public void setUp() {
        calculator = new Calculator();
    }

    @Test
    public void testAdd() {
        assertEquals(5, calculator.add(2, 3));
    }

    @Test
    public void testSubtract() {
        assertEquals(1, calculator.subtract(3, 2));
    }
}
```

JUnit's simplicity and flexibility make it a popular choice for unit testing in Java.

2. Mockito for Mocking Dependencies

Mockito is a mocking framework that allows developers to isolate units of code by creating mock objects. Mocks are useful for testing classes with dependencies, especially when those dependencies are complex or have side effects (e.g., database calls, network requests).

- **Mocks**: Substitute dependencies with mock objects.

- **Stubbing**: Define the behavior of a mock in specific test scenarios.

- **Verification**: Ensure certain interactions with the mock occurred.

Example of Mockito for Dependency Injection:

Suppose we have a UserService class that depends on a UserRepository.

```
import static org.mockito.Mockito.*;

import org.junit.jupiter.api.BeforeEach;

import org.junit.jupiter.api.Test;

import org.mockito.InjectMocks;

import org.mockito.Mock;
```

```java
import org.mockito.MockitoAnnotations;

public class UserServiceTest {
    @Mock
    private UserRepository userRepository;

    @InjectMocks
    private UserService userService;

    @BeforeEach
    public void setUp() {
        MockitoAnnotations.openMocks(this);
    }

    @Test
    public void testFindUserById() {

when(userRepository.findById(1)).thenReturn(new
User(1, "Alice"));

        User user = userService.findUserById(1);
```

```
    assertEquals("Alice", user.getName());

    verify(userRepository).findById(1);
  }
}
```

With Mockito, we can mock the UserRepository to control its behavior, isolate the UserService, and verify interactions.

3. Integration Testing

Integration testing verifies the interaction between multiple components, such as database access, external APIs, or other system services. Integration tests often use a different environment than unit tests to include real databases or external services.

Example of an Integration Test with Spring Boot:

Spring Boot provides tools for easy integration testing with an embedded application context, allowing developers to test end-to-end flows.

```
import org.junit.jupiter.api.Test;
```

```java
import
org.springframework.boot.test.context.SpringBootTest
;

import
org.springframework.beans.factory.annotation.Autowir
ed;

import static org.assertj.core.api.Assertions.assertThat;


@SpringBootTest
public class UserServiceIntegrationTest {

    @Autowired
    private UserService userService;

    @Test
    public void testCreateUser() {
        User user = new User("Alice");
        User createdUser = userService.createUser(user);
        assertThat(createdUser.getId()).isNotNull();

assertThat(createdUser.getName()).isEqualTo("Alice")
;
    }
```

```
}
```

Using Spring Boot's @SpringBootTest, this integration test starts an embedded context and uses real application components to verify functionality.

Scenario: Testing a Complex Distributed System

Let's apply these testing strategies to a complex distributed system, such as a microservices-based e-commerce application with multiple services that interact through APIs.

Scenario Overview

In this example, the e-commerce application has the following services:

1. **User Service**: Manages user accounts and authentication.

2. **Product Service**: Manages product information.

3. **Order Service**: Handles order processing, integrates with Payment and Inventory services.

Each service is independent but communicates with others, requiring comprehensive testing to ensure correct integration.

Step-by-Step Testing Strategy

1. **Unit Testing with JUnit and Mockito**

Start by writing unit tests for each service. Use Mockito to mock dependencies and isolate each component.

Example: Testing the OrderService to verify that it correctly processes orders.

```
@Test
public void testPlaceOrder() {

when(paymentService.processPayment(any())).thenRe
turn(true);

when(inventoryService.checkStock(anyString())).then
Return(true);


    boolean success = orderService.placeOrder(new
Order(...));
    assertTrue(success);
```

```
verify(paymentService).processPayment(any());

verify(inventoryService).checkStock(anyString());
```

}

2. Integration Testing Between Services

Integration tests verify that services interact as expected. Use **Spring Boot Test** for testing each service in isolation, and **WireMock** or **MockServer** to simulate HTTP requests to other services.

Example: Testing that the OrderService correctly interacts with PaymentService and InventoryService.

```
@Autowired
private OrderService orderService;


@MockBean
private PaymentService paymentService;


@MockBean
private InventoryService inventoryService;


@Test
public void testPlaceOrderWithRealDependencies() {
```

```java
when(paymentService.processPayment(any())).thenRe
turn(true);

when(inventoryService.checkStock(anyString())).then
Return(true);


    Order order = new Order(...);

    boolean result = orderService.placeOrder(order);

    assertTrue(result);
}
```

3. End-to-End Testing with API Calls

End-to-End (E2E) testing simulates real user interactions by executing the entire workflow of creating a user, browsing products, and placing an order.

Use tools like **Postman** or **REST-assured** for API-level tests, or **Selenium** for UI-based tests if a front-end is available.

Example of an API-Level E2E Test with REST-assured:

```java
import io.restassured.RestAssured;
import static io.restassured.RestAssured.*;
```

```java
import static org.hamcrest.Matchers.*;

@Test
public void endToEndOrderPlacement() {
    RestAssured.baseURI = "http://localhost:8080";

    // Step 1: Create User
    int userId = given()
        .contentType("application/json")
        .body(new User("Alice"))
        .post("/api/users")
        .then()
        .statusCode(201)
        .extract()
        .path("id");

    // Step 2: Place Order
    given()
        .contentType("application/json")
        .body(new Order(userId, "product123", 100))
        .post("/api/orders")
```

```
.then()

.statusCode(200)

.body("status", equalTo("success"));

}
```

4. Load Testing with JMeter

To test scalability and ensure each service handles high traffic, use **Apache JMeter** or **Gatling**. These tools simulate multiple concurrent requests to check for performance bottlenecks.

5. Debugging Failed Tests

When tests fail, use debugging tools such as **IDE Debuggers** for unit tests, **logs** for API testing, and **distributed tracing** tools like **Jaeger** or **Zipkin** for complex, distributed services.

Conclusion

Testing and debugging are crucial to ensuring the reliability and resilience of Java applications, especially in complex, distributed systems. In this chapter, we covered the principles of Test-Driven Development (TDD) and Behavior-Driven Development (BDD), discussed advanced testing techniques using JUnit, Mockito, and integration testing, and applied these methods to test a distributed e-commerce system.

By mastering testing and debugging strategies, developers can confidently build applications that scale, handle errors gracefully, and meet user expectations for quality and performance. These practices ultimately reduce time spent on fixing bugs and increase overall development efficiency, making them indispensable in professional software engineering.

Chapter 18: Security Best Practices in Java Applications

In today's digital landscape, security is a critical component of any software application, especially in sensitive domains like e-commerce, finance, and healthcare. Java applications are no exception, as they often handle sensitive data that needs robust protection from threats such as unauthorized access, data breaches, and other cyberattacks. This chapter explores essential security best practices, Java security features, secure coding principles, and demonstrates a practical example of implementing secure login and payment processing in an e-commerce application.

Implementing Security Best Practices: Data Protection, Secure APIs, and Authentication

Security best practices are guidelines and strategies designed to protect applications and data from potential threats. Following these principles ensures that your Java application is built with a security-first mindset, reducing the risk of vulnerabilities.

1. Data Protection

Data protection is vital in securing an application, especially when handling sensitive information like passwords, payment details, and personal data. Key practices include encryption, hashing, and data masking.

- **Encryption**: Encrypt sensitive data both in transit (using SSL/TLS for network transmission) and at rest (using database encryption) to prevent unauthorized access. Java offers built-in support for encryption algorithms like AES and RSA.

Example of AES Encryption:

```
import javax.crypto.Cipher;

import javax.crypto.KeyGenerator;

import javax.crypto.SecretKey;


public class EncryptionExample {

    public static void main(String[] args) throws Exception {
```

```java
    KeyGenerator keyGen =
KeyGenerator.getInstance("AES");

    keyGen.init(128);

    SecretKey secretKey = keyGen.generateKey();


    Cipher cipher = Cipher.getInstance("AES");

    cipher.init(Cipher.ENCRYPT_MODE,
secretKey);


    byte[] encryptedData =
cipher.doFinal("SensitiveData".getBytes());

    System.out.println("Encrypted Data: " + new
String(encryptedData));

    }

}
```

- **Hashing**: Hash passwords and other sensitive information to avoid storing raw data. Use secure algorithms like **bcrypt** or **PBKDF2** to protect passwords.

Example of Hashing with bcrypt (Using Spring Security):

```java
import
org.springframework.security.crypto.bcrypt.BCryptPas
swordEncoder;


public class HashingExample {

   public static void main(String[] args) {

     BCryptPasswordEncoder encoder = new
BCryptPasswordEncoder();

     String hashedPassword =
encoder.encode("password123");

     System.out.println("Hashed Password: " +
hashedPassword);

   }
}
```

- **Data Masking**: Mask sensitive data, such as showing only the last four digits of a credit card number, to prevent exposure.

2. Secure APIs

Secure APIs are essential for protecting data and functionality from unauthorized access. Implement these security measures:

- **API Authentication and Authorization**: Enforce strong authentication (e.g., OAuth 2.0, JWT) and authorization mechanisms for API access.

- **Rate Limiting**: Limit the number of requests to prevent abuse and reduce the impact of potential DoS (Denial of Service) attacks.

- **Input Validation**: Validate all incoming data to protect against SQL injection, cross-site scripting (XSS), and other injection attacks.

Example of Secure API Authentication with JWT (JSON Web Tokens):

1. **Generate JWT**:

```
import io.jsonwebtoken.Jwts;

import io.jsonwebtoken.SignatureAlgorithm;


public class JwtUtil {

    private static final String SECRET_KEY = "mySecretKey";


    public static String generateToken(String username) {

        return Jwts.builder()

            .setSubject(username)

            .signWith(SignatureAlgorithm.HS256, SECRET_KEY)
```

```
        .compact();

    }

}
```

2. Validate JWT:

```
public boolean validateToken(String token) {

    try {

Jwts.parser().setSigningKey(SECRET_KEY).parseCla
imsJws(token);

        return true;

    } catch (Exception e) {

        return false;

    }

}
```

3. Authentication and Authorization

Authentication and authorization form the foundation of application security, controlling who can access which resources.

- **Authentication**: Verify users' identities before granting access. Use strong authentication methods like multi-factor authentication (MFA) and tokens (e.g., JWT, OAuth) to secure login systems.

- **Authorization**: Define and enforce access control policies, ensuring that users can only access resources and perform actions they are permitted to.

Role-Based Access Control Example with Spring Security:

```
import org.springframework.context.annotation.Configuration;
import org.springframework.security.config.annotation.authentication.builders.AuthenticationManagerBuilder;
import org.springframework.security.config.annotation.web.builders.HttpSecurity;
import org.springframework.security.config.annotation.web.configuration.WebSecurityConfigurerAdapter;


@Configuration
public class SecurityConfig extends WebSecurityConfigurerAdapter {
```

```java
@Override

protected void
configure(AuthenticationManagerBuilder auth) throws
Exception {

    auth.inMemoryAuthentication()

.withUser("user").password("{noop}password").roles(
"USER")

        .and()

.withUser("admin").password("{noop}admin").roles("
ADMIN");
    }


    @Override

    protected void configure(HttpSecurity http) throws
Exception {
        http.authorizeRequests()

            .antMatchers("/admin/**").hasRole("ADMIN")

            .antMatchers("/user/**").hasRole("USER")

            .and().formLogin();
    }
```

```
}
```

In this example, users are authenticated with in-memory credentials, and authorization rules are defined based on user roles.

Java Security Features and Secure Coding Principles

Java offers built-in security features and practices that protect against common vulnerabilities. Following secure coding principles enhances security and reduces risks.

1. Java Security Features

Java includes several features for application security:

- **Java Cryptography Architecture (JCA)**: Provides a framework for encryption, hashing, and secure random number generation. Use the javax.crypto package for cryptographic operations.

- **Java Secure Socket Extension (JSSE)**: Supports secure communication over SSL/TLS, securing data in transit.

- **Java Authentication and Authorization Service (JAAS)**: Provides a framework for authentication and authorization in Java applications.

2. Secure Coding Principles

To reduce vulnerabilities, follow secure coding principles when writing Java code:

- **Least Privilege**: Assign the minimum permissions required for each component.

- **Fail-Safe Defaults**: Configure applications to deny access by default, requiring explicit permission.

- **Input Validation and Output Encoding**: Validate all input data and encode output to prevent injection attacks.

- **Avoid Hardcoding Secrets**: Store sensitive data, such as API keys and passwords, in secure storage, not in source code.

- **Exception Handling**: Avoid disclosing sensitive information in exception messages. Handle exceptions properly to prevent information leakage.

Example of Input Validation to Prevent SQL Injection:

Instead of concatenating strings in SQL queries, use prepared statements:

java

```java
public User findUserByUsername(String username) {

    String sql = "SELECT * FROM users WHERE
username = ?";

    try (PreparedStatement stmt =
connection.prepareStatement(sql)) {

        stmt.setString(1, username);

        ResultSet rs = stmt.executeQuery();

        // process result

    } catch (SQLException e) {

        // handle exception

    }

}
```

Using prepared statements prevents SQL injection by safely handling special characters.

Example: Secure Login and Payment Processing in an E-Commerce Platform

Let's put these security principles into practice by building a secure login and payment processing flow for an e-commerce application.

1. Secure Login Implementation

The login system should authenticate users securely, using hashing for password storage, multi-factor authentication, and token-based sessions.

Step 1: Password Hashing and Storage

Store hashed passwords instead of plain text. Use **BCrypt** to hash passwords, as it includes a built-in salt and is resistant to brute-force attacks.

Password Hashing with BCrypt:

```
import
org.springframework.security.crypto.bcrypt.BCryptPas
swordEncoder;


public class UserService {

    private BCryptPasswordEncoder encoder = new
BCryptPasswordEncoder();
```

```java
    public void registerUser(String username, String
rawPassword) {

        String hashedPassword =
encoder.encode(rawPassword);

        // Save username and hashedPassword to the
database

    }

}
```

Step 2: Implementing JWT Authentication

After successful login, issue a JWT to the client, which
will be sent in subsequent requests as a token.

1. **Generate JWT on Login**:

```java
public String authenticate(String username, String
password) {

    // Verify username and password

    return JwtUtil.generateToken(username);

}
```

2. **Validate JWT on Requests**:

In each request, the client sends the JWT in the header.
Verify the token to ensure it's valid before proceeding.

```java
@GetMapping("/profile")

public ResponseEntity<?>
getUserProfile(@RequestHeader("Authorization")
String token) {

    if (!JwtUtil.validateToken(token)) {

        return
ResponseEntity.status(HttpStatus.UNAUTHORIZED).
build();

    }

    // Process request

}
```

Step 3: Multi-Factor Authentication (MFA)

Integrate MFA by generating a one-time code that
users need to enter along with their password.

1. **Send OTP to User**: Upon successful password
   validation, generate a random OTP and send it
   via email or SMS.

2. **Validate OTP**: Require users to enter the OTP
   to complete the login process.

2. Secure Payment Processing

In payment processing, security is critical to protect
sensitive financial information. Use HTTPS,

encryption, tokenization, and secure payment gateways.

Step 1: Using a Payment Gateway

Use third-party payment providers (e.g., Stripe, PayPal) that handle payment data securely. This offloads payment security to a PCI-DSS compliant service.

Example Payment Integration with Stripe (simplified):

```java
import com.stripe.Stripe;
import com.stripe.model.PaymentIntent;

public class PaymentService {

    public PaymentService() {
        Stripe.apiKey = "sk_test_12345";
    }

    public String createPayment(double amount, String currency) {
```

```java
        Map<String, Object> params = new
HashMap<>();

        params.put("amount", (int) (amount * 100)); //
Amount in cents

        params.put("currency", currency);

        params.put("payment_method_types",
Arrays.asList("card"));


        PaymentIntent paymentIntent =
PaymentIntent.create(params);

        return paymentIntent.getClientSecret();

    }

}
```

In this example, the createPayment method generates a payment intent and returns a client secret, allowing the client to complete the payment securely on the client side.

Step 2: Encrypting Payment Data

If you handle sensitive payment data directly, use strong encryption to protect it both in transit and at rest.

```java
public String encryptCardNumber(String cardNumber)
throws Exception {
```

```java
Cipher cipher = Cipher.getInstance("AES");

cipher.init(Cipher.ENCRYPT_MODE, secretKey);

byte[] encryptedData =
cipher.doFinal(cardNumber.getBytes());

return
Base64.getEncoder().encodeToString(encryptedData);

}
```

Step 3: Secure Order Processing Workflow

1. **Tokenize Sensitive Data**: For recurring payments, store a token rather than sensitive data like credit card numbers.

2. **Validate Orders**: Verify that payment is authorized before processing an order.

3. **Audit Logs**: Log all payment actions, including user IDs and order details, for accountability and security audits.

Conclusion

Security is a fundamental aspect of Java application development, especially in areas handling sensitive user data, authentication, and financial transactions. In this chapter, we explored best practices for data protection, secure APIs, and authentication, examined Java's security features and secure coding principles, and applied these practices in a practical example of secure login and payment processing for an e-commerce application.

Implementing security best practices minimizes risks and builds trust, ensuring that applications are resilient against vulnerabilities and potential attacks. Following these principles is essential for delivering safe, reliable, and user-friendly software in an increasingly security-conscious digital environment.

Part 5
Java in Modern Architectures and Emerging Technologies

Chapter 19: Java in Cloud Computing and Serverless Environments

Cloud computing has revolutionized how applications are deployed and scaled, offering flexibility, cost-efficiency, and powerful resources for developers. Java, with its robust ecosystem and flexibility, is a prime choice for cloud-native development. In this chapter, we explore how to deploy Java applications across popular cloud platforms like **AWS**, **Azure**, and **Google Cloud**, discuss essential cloud-native design principles such as serverless functions and containerization, and conclude with a practical example of a serverless Java application for real-time image processing.

Deploying Java Applications on AWS, Azure, and Google Cloud

Each of the major cloud providers—Amazon Web Services (AWS), Microsoft Azure, and Google Cloud Platform (GCP)—offers unique features and tools to deploy Java applications efficiently. Here's how to get started with deploying Java applications on each platform, leveraging their managed services, scaling, and cloud-native tools.

1. Deploying Java Applications on AWS

AWS provides multiple services for deploying Java applications, from serverless functions to container orchestration:

- **Amazon Elastic Beanstalk**: This Platform-as-a-Service (PaaS) is ideal for deploying Java applications quickly without manually managing the underlying infrastructure. Elastic Beanstalk supports Java applications out of the box, handles load balancing, auto-scaling, and provides easy integration with other AWS services.

- **Amazon Elastic Kubernetes Service (EKS)**: A managed Kubernetes service where you can run containerized Java applications, ideal for microservices architectures.

- **AWS Lambda**: A serverless compute service that allows developers to run Java code in response to events without provisioning servers.

Deploying a Java Application on AWS Elastic Beanstalk:

1. **Package the Application**: Package your Java application into a .jar or .war file.

2. **Create an Environment**: In the AWS Console, navigate to **Elastic Beanstalk**, create a new environment, and choose Java as the platform.

3. **Upload and Deploy**: Upload the packaged file, and Elastic Beanstalk automatically handles provisioning, scaling, and monitoring.

Example Commands Using AWS CLI:

bash

```
# Initialize Elastic Beanstalk application
eb init -p java-11 my-java-app


# Create and deploy an environment
eb create my-env
eb deploy
```

2. Deploying Java Applications on Microsoft Azure

Azure offers multiple managed services for Java applications, enabling Java developers to build and deploy highly scalable applications in the cloud:

- **Azure App Service**: A fully managed platform for deploying Java web applications with built-in load balancing and scaling.

- **Azure Kubernetes Service (AKS)**: Managed Kubernetes, allowing you to deploy containerized Java applications and take advantage of the microservices architecture.

- **Azure Functions**: A serverless compute solution that allows Java applications to run on-demand in response to events.

Deploying a Java Application on Azure App Service:

1. **Create an App Service**: In the Azure portal, create a new App Service and choose Java as the runtime stack.

2. **Deploy Using Azure CLI**: Package your Java application, then deploy using the Azure CLI.

Example Azure CLI Commands:

bash

```
# Create App Service plan and Java web app

az appservice plan create --name myAppServicePlan --resource-group myResourceGroup --sku B1

az webapp create --name myJavaApp --plan myAppServicePlan --runtime "JAVA|11" --resource-group myResourceGroup


# Deploy application

az webapp deploy --resource-group myResourceGroup --name myJavaApp --src-path path/to/app.jar
```

3. Deploying Java Applications on Google Cloud Platform (GCP)

Google Cloud provides several tools and services for deploying Java applications, tailored for both managed and containerized environments:

- **Google App Engine**: A PaaS solution that provides automatic scaling and load balancing for Java applications, simplifying deployment.

- **Google Kubernetes Engine (GKE)**: A managed Kubernetes service, ideal for deploying containerized Java microservices with powerful orchestration and scaling capabilities.

- **Google Cloud Functions**: A serverless compute service, best suited for lightweight Java functions that run in response to events.

Deploying a Java Application on Google App Engine:

1. **Create a Configuration File (app.yaml)**: Configure the application's runtime and instance settings.

yaml

runtime: java11

instance_class: F1

2. **Deploy Using gcloud CLI**:

bash

gcloud app deploy

This command automatically deploys your Java application to App Engine, where it scales based on demand and receives traffic through Google's load balancing.

Cloud-Native Design, Serverless Functions, and Containerization

To fully leverage the benefits of the cloud, applications need to follow cloud-native design principles. Here, we explore the fundamentals of cloud-native design, serverless functions, and containerization.

1. Cloud-Native Design Principles

Cloud-native applications are designed to be resilient, scalable, and flexible to adapt to modern cloud infrastructure. Key principles include:

- **Microservices Architecture**: Decompose applications into loosely coupled services, allowing independent development, deployment, and scaling of each service. This architecture is foundational to building resilient, scalable applications.

- **API-First Design**: Adopt an API-centric approach to standardize communication between services, making integration easier and more reliable.

- **Statelessness**: Stateless applications do not rely on server sessions or saved states. This allows them to scale easily as any instance can handle any request, as session data is stored in external data stores.

- **Automation and Observability**: Automate deployments, monitoring, and scaling through CI/CD pipelines and tools like Prometheus or Grafana to ensure application reliability.

2. Serverless Functions

Serverless computing allows applications to execute code in response to events without managing servers. Java is widely supported in serverless environments through services like **AWS Lambda**, **Azure Functions**, and **Google Cloud Functions**.

- **Event-Driven Execution**: Serverless functions respond to events such as HTTP requests, database updates, or file uploads.

- **Auto-Scaling**: Serverless platforms scale automatically to handle any load, charging only for actual usage.

- **Short-Lived Execution**: Ideal for tasks that complete quickly; long-running tasks can be managed with serverless orchestration services like AWS Step Functions or Azure Durable Functions.

Example AWS Lambda Function in Java:

```
import
com.amazonaws.services.lambda.runtime.Context;
```

```java
import
com.amazonaws.services.lambda.runtime.RequestHan
dler;

import java.util.Map;


public class HelloLambda implements
RequestHandler<Map<String, String>, String> {

    @Override

    public String handleRequest(Map<String, String>
input, Context context) {

        return "Hello, " + input.get("name");

    }

}
```

This function, triggered by an event (e.g., HTTP request), responds with a greeting. You can deploy it using the AWS Console, CLI, or SDK.

3. Containerization with Docker and Kubernetes

Containerization packages applications and their dependencies, ensuring consistent behavior across environments. Docker is the most popular containerization tool, while Kubernetes is used for orchestrating and managing containers in production.

- **Docker**: Docker images encapsulate the application, making it portable and consistent across deployments. Docker containers are compatible with cloud services like AWS ECS, Azure Container Instances, and Google Cloud Run.

Dockerfile Example for Java Application:

dockerfile

```
FROM openjdk:11-jre-slim
COPY target/app.jar /app/app.jar
ENTRYPOINT ["java", "-jar", "/app/app.jar"]
```

- **Kubernetes**: Kubernetes manages containers in clusters, handling deployment, scaling, and load balancing. Kubernetes clusters are available on AWS (EKS), Azure (AKS), and GCP (GKE).

Kubernetes Deployment Example for Java Application:

yaml

```
apiVersion: apps/v1
kind: Deployment
metadata:
  name: java-app
spec:
  replicas: 3
```

```yaml
  selector:
    matchLabels:
      app: java-app
  template:
    metadata:
      labels:
        app: java-app
    spec:
      containers:
      - name: java-app
        image: my-java-app-image
        ports:
        - containerPort: 8080
```

This deployment defines a Kubernetes cluster with three replicas of the Java application, providing high availability and scalability.

Example: Serverless Java Application for Real-Time Image Processing

Let's build a serverless Java application that performs real-time image processing on uploaded files. This example leverages **AWS Lambda** and **Amazon S3** to create a cost-effective, scalable solution.

Scenario Overview

1. **Trigger**: When an image is uploaded to an Amazon S3 bucket, it triggers a Lambda function.

2. **Process**: The Lambda function resizes the image to a specific resolution.

3. **Save**: The processed image is saved back to a designated S3 bucket for further use.

Step-by-Step Implementation

Step 1: Set Up S3 Buckets

Create two S3 buckets:

- source-bucket: Stores the original images.

- processed-bucket: Stores the resized images after processing.

Step 2: Define the Lambda Function

The Lambda function will be triggered by S3 events, process the image, and save it to the target bucket.

Lambda Function Code for Image Processing:

```java
import
com.amazonaws.services.lambda.runtime.Context;

import
com.amazonaws.services.lambda.runtime.events.S3Event;

import com.amazonaws.services.s3.AmazonS3;

import
com.amazonaws.services.s3.AmazonS3ClientBuilder;

import com.amazonaws.services.s3.model.S3Object;

import java.awt.image.BufferedImage;

import javax.imageio.ImageIO;

import java.io.InputStream;

import java.io.ByteArrayOutputStream;

import
com.amazonaws.services.s3.model.ObjectMetadata;

import java.io.ByteArrayInputStream;


public class ImageProcessorLambda {
```

```java
    private final AmazonS3 s3Client =
AmazonS3ClientBuilder.defaultClient();


    public void handleRequest(S3Event event, Context
context) {
        event.getRecords().forEach(record -> {
            String bucketName =
record.getS3().getBucket().getName();
            String objectKey =
record.getS3().getObject().getKey();


            try (S3Object s3Object =
s3Client.getObject(bucketName, objectKey);
                 InputStream objectData =
s3Object.getObjectContent()) {


                BufferedImage image =
ImageIO.read(objectData);
                BufferedImage resizedImage =
resizeImage(image, 200, 200);


                ByteArrayOutputStream os = new
ByteArrayOutputStream();
                ImageIO.write(resizedImage, "jpg", os);
```

```java
            byte[] imageBytes = os.toByteArray();


            ObjectMetadata metadata = new
ObjectMetadata();

metadata.setContentLength(imageBytes.length);
            ByteArrayInputStream
byteArrayInputStream = new
ByteArrayInputStream(imageBytes);


            s3Client.putObject("processed-bucket",
"processed-" + objectKey, byteArrayInputStream,
metadata);
        } catch (Exception e) {

            context.getLogger().log("Error processing
image: " + e.getMessage());

        }
    });
}


    private BufferedImage resizeImage(BufferedImage
originalImage, int width, int height) {
```

```
    BufferedImage resizedImage = new
BufferedImage(width, height,
originalImage.getType());


resizedImage.getGraphics().drawImage(originalImage,
0, 0, width, height, null);

    return resizedImage;

  }

}
```

- **Event Handler**: The handleRequest method receives the S3 event, retrieves the image, and resizes it.

- **Image Processing**: The resizeImage method scales the image to the desired dimensions.

- **Saving**: The processed image is saved to the processed-bucket.

Step 3: Configure the Lambda Function to Trigger on S3 Events

In the AWS Console:

1. Set up the Lambda function.

2. Add an S3 trigger to the source-bucket to invoke the function on ObjectCreated events.

Step 4: Test the Application

Upload an image to the source-bucket and confirm that the Lambda function processes it. The resized image should appear in the processed-bucket.

Conclusion

This chapter covered the essentials of deploying Java applications in cloud and serverless environments, along with an example of using AWS Lambda for real-time image processing. By embracing cloud-native principles, serverless functions, and containerization, Java developers can create scalable, flexible, and efficient applications for today's technology landscape. These skills and practices will empower you to build robust applications capable of meeting the demands of modern users.

Chapter 20: Java for IoT and Edge Computing

The Internet of Things (IoT) and edge computing have transformed how devices interact and process data. By processing data closer to where it's generated, edge computing reduces latency and bandwidth requirements, which is critical in time-sensitive applications such as real-time monitoring, industrial automation, and autonomous vehicles. Java is well-suited for IoT and edge computing, offering portability, reliability, and a vast ecosystem of libraries and frameworks. In this chapter, we explore building low-latency Java applications for IoT and edge devices, integrating Java into resource-constrained environments, and conclude with a practical example of a real-time monitoring system for IoT sensors.

Building Low-Latency Java Applications for IoT and Edge Devices

IoT and edge applications often require low-latency processing to handle real-time data effectively. Java provides tools and techniques for achieving low latency while ensuring reliability in edge computing environments

1. Requirements for Low-Latency IoT Applications

To meet the demands of IoT and edge devices, applications need to minimize processing delays. Key requirements for low-latency IoT applications include:

- **Real-Time Data Processing**: Applications must process data as soon as it's received, especially in time-sensitive applications like industrial monitoring.

- **Efficient Resource Usage**: IoT and edge devices often have limited processing power, memory, and storage, requiring optimized code.

- **Resilience and Fault Tolerance**: Edge devices may operate in harsh environments where connectivity is unreliable, so applications must handle intermittent connectivity gracefully.

2. Java Techniques for Low Latency

To optimize Java applications for low-latency environments, we can use techniques like Just-In-Time (JIT) compilation, efficient garbage collection, and asynchronous processing.

- **JIT Compilation**: Java's Just-In-Time (JIT) compiler compiles frequently used bytecode to native code at runtime, optimizing performance. For edge applications, enabling JIT compilation can reduce latency after the initial warm-up phase.

- **Efficient Garbage Collection**: Use garbage collection (GC) configurations suitable for real-time and low-latency applications. The **G1 Garbage Collector** and **Z Garbage Collector (ZGC)** are known for low pause times, which can improve responsiveness in IoT applications.

- **Asynchronous Processing**: Use asynchronous programming with Java's CompletableFuture, ExecutorService, or reactive libraries like **Project Reactor** to handle concurrent tasks, which helps manage high data ingestion rates typical of IoT environments.

Example of Asynchronous Data Processing Using CompletableFuture:

```java
import java.util.concurrent.CompletableFuture;

public class DataProcessor {
    public CompletableFuture<Void>
processDataAsync(String data) {
        return CompletableFuture.runAsync(() -> {
            // Process data
            System.out.println("Processing data: " + data);
        });
    }

    public static void main(String[] args) {
        DataProcessor processor = new DataProcessor();

processor.processDataAsync("sensor_data").thenRun((
) -> System.out.println("Data processed."));
    }
}
```

This asynchronous approach reduces processing delays and enables handling multiple data streams simultaneously, which is useful in edge computing.

Integrating Java in Resource-Constrained Environments

Java applications in IoT and edge computing often need to run on resource-constrained devices, such as sensors or small gateways. To make Java efficient in such environments, special configurations and lightweight versions of the JVM are used.

1. Lightweight Java Runtimes

Java applications running on constrained devices benefit from smaller, optimized JVMs. Here are some popular options:

- **GraalVM**: A high-performance runtime that allows applications to be compiled into native executables, reducing startup time and memory usage. GraalVM is suitable for IoT and edge applications as it minimizes resource overhead and enhances performance.

- **Eclipse MicroProfile**: A framework for building microservices in Java, optimized for low-resource environments. It provides a lean set of APIs to build microservices while keeping memory usage low.

- **Embedded JVMs**: Java SE Embedded and other embedded JVMs are specifically designed to run on devices with limited processing power. These JVMs can be customized to include only the necessary modules, reducing memory usage.

2. Java Frameworks for IoT and Edge Devices

Several Java frameworks are specifically designed for IoT and edge computing, making it easier to interface with hardware and process sensor data.

- **Eclipse IoT**: Eclipse IoT is an open-source initiative that provides Java libraries for IoT applications. Projects like **Eclipse Kura** (IoT gateway framework) and **Eclipse Paho** (MQTT messaging) simplify IoT development by providing APIs to connect to devices, manage communication, and process data at the edge.

- **Apache Edgent**: Edgent is a lightweight analytics framework designed for edge devices, allowing developers to run analytics on data directly at the source. It supports stream processing and can be integrated with cloud platforms.

Example of Using Eclipse Paho for MQTT Messaging:

MQTT (Message Queuing Telemetry Transport) is a lightweight messaging protocol commonly used in IoT. The following example demonstrates publishing data to an MQTT broker with Eclipse Paho.

```java
import org.eclipse.paho.client.mqttv3.MqttClient;

import org.eclipse.paho.client.mqttv3.MqttException;

import org.eclipse.paho.client.mqttv3.MqttMessage;


public class SensorPublisher {

    public static void main(String[] args) throws
MqttException {

        String broker = "tcp://mqtt.example.com:1883";

        String clientId = "sensorPublisher";

        MqttClient client = new MqttClient(broker,
clientId);

        client.connect();


        String topic = "sensor/temperature";

        String payload = "23.4";

        MqttMessage message = new
MqttMessage(payload.getBytes());

        client.publish(topic, message);

        System.out.println("Message published to topic: "
+ topic);
```

```
    client.disconnect();
  }
}
```

This example publishes temperature data to an MQTT broker, a common setup in IoT for real-time data communication between devices.

Scenario: Real-Time Monitoring System for IoT Sensors

Let's apply the concepts covered so far by designing a real-time monitoring system for IoT sensors. This scenario involves a distributed setup where sensors send data to edge devices, which process the data locally and send relevant information to the cloud for further analysis.

System Requirements

The system will monitor temperature and humidity data in a warehouse. Each sensor collects data every few seconds and sends it to an edge device. The edge device processes the data and raises alerts if temperature or humidity exceed safe levels.

Key features include:

1. **Low-Latency Processing**: Process data in real-time to detect anomalies and trigger alerts immediately.

2. **Efficient Communication**: Use MQTT for lightweight messaging between sensors and edge devices.

3. **Local Storage and Aggregation**: Store and aggregate data at the edge to reduce cloud communication.

System Architecture

1. **Sensors**: Collect temperature and humidity data and send it to edge devices over MQTT.

2. **Edge Device**: Runs a Java application that receives data, processes it, raises alerts if necessary, and stores aggregated data locally.

3. **Cloud Service**: Receives summarized data from the edge device and provides a web dashboard for monitoring.

Step-by-Step Implementation

Step 1: Set Up Sensor Data Publishing

Simulate sensor data using an MQTT client in Java (using Eclipse Paho). Each sensor will publish data to a topic on the edge device's MQTT broker.

Sensor Data Publisher (Simulated):

```java
import org.eclipse.paho.client.mqttv3.MqttClient;
import org.eclipse.paho.client.mqttv3.MqttMessage;

import java.util.Random;

public class SensorSimulator {
    private static final String BROKER_URL =
"tcp://localhost:1883";
    private static final String TOPIC =
"warehouse/sensors";

    public static void main(String[] args) throws
Exception {
        MqttClient client = new
MqttClient(BROKER_URL,
MqttClient.generateClientId());
        client.connect();

        Random random = new Random();
        while (true) {
            double temperature = 20 +
random.nextDouble() * 10; // Random temperature
between 20 and 30
```

```java
        double humidity = 40 + random.nextDouble() *
20;    // Random humidity between 40 and 60

        String data = String.format("{\"temperature\":
%.2f, \"humidity\": %.2f}", temperature, humidity);


        MqttMessage message = new
MqttMessage(data.getBytes());

        client.publish(TOPIC, message);

        System.out.println("Data published: " + data);


        Thread.sleep(5000); // Publish every 5 seconds

    }

  }

}
```

This simulated sensor sends random temperature and humidity values every five seconds to an MQTT broker running on the edge device.

Step 2: Set Up Data Processing on the Edge Device

On the edge device, we create a Java application that subscribes to the sensor data topic, processes incoming data, and raises alerts if values exceed safe thresholds.

Edge Device Processor:

java

```java
import org.eclipse.paho.client.mqttv3.*;

public class EdgeDeviceProcessor implements
MqttCallback {

    private static final String BROKER_URL =
"tcp://localhost:1883";

    private static final String TOPIC =
"warehouse/sensors";


    public static void main(String[] args) throws
Exception {

        MqttClient client = new
MqttClient(BROKER_URL,
MqttClient.generateClientId());

        client.setCallback(new EdgeDeviceProcessor());

        client.connect();

        client.subscribe(TOPIC);

        System.out.println("Subscribed to topic: " +
TOPIC);

    }


    @Override
```

```java
public void connectionLost(Throwable cause) {

    System.out.println("Connection lost: " +
cause.getMessage());

  }


  @Override
  public void messageArrived(String topic,
MqttMessage message) throws Exception {

    String payload = new
String(message.getPayload());

    System.out.println("Data received: " + payload);


    // Parse data and check thresholds

    double temperature = parseTemperature(payload);

    double humidity = parseHumidity(payload);


    if (temperature > 28) {

        System.out.println("ALERT: High temperature
detected!");

    }

    if (humidity > 50) {
```

```java
        System.out.println("ALERT: High humidity
detected!");
    }
  }


    private double parseTemperature(String payload) {
        // Parse JSON or extract temperature value
        return
Double.parseDouble(payload.split(",")[0].split(":")[1]);
    }


    private double parseHumidity(String payload) {
        // Parse JSON or extract humidity value
        return
Double.parseDouble(payload.split(",")[1].split(":")[1]);
    }


    @Override
    public void deliveryComplete(IMqttDeliveryToken
token) {}
}
```

The edge processor subscribes to the topic, processes each message, and checks if temperature or humidity exceed safe thresholds, triggering alerts if necessary.

Step 3: Data Aggregation and Cloud Communication

For long-term storage and analysis, the edge device can aggregate data (e.g., calculate hourly averages) and send summaries to a cloud service.

- **Data Aggregation**: The edge processor stores data locally and calculates averages every hour.

- **Cloud Upload**: Aggregated data is sent to the cloud using HTTP or MQTT, enabling remote monitoring.

Step 4: Cloud Monitoring Dashboard

The cloud service receives data and displays it on a dashboard. Tools like **Grafana** or **Elasticsearch** can visualize real-time and historical data, providing insights into warehouse conditions.

Conclusion

Java is a powerful platform for IoT and edge computing, offering robust performance, portability, and a rich ecosystem. In this chapter, we explored how to build low-latency Java applications for IoT, optimize Java for resource-constrained environments, and connect to IoT sensors using protocols like MQTT.

The example of a real-time monitoring system illustrates how Java applications can process data at the edge, raising alerts in real time and reducing latency. As IoT and edge computing continue to evolve, mastering Java for these environments will empower developers to create responsive, reliable, and secure applications that bring data processing closer to the source, improving both efficiency and resilience.

Chapter 21: Future Trends in Java Development

Java has been a dominant force in software development for over two decades, and its adaptability has kept it relevant across multiple technology waves, from enterprise software to cloud-native applications. Today, Java continues to evolve to meet the demands of modern software development in fields like artificial intelligence (AI), blockchain, Internet of Things (IoT), and microservices. In this final chapter, we explore emerging trends and upcoming Java features, Java's evolving role in areas like blockchain and AI, and provide final thoughts on the importance of continuous learning in this rapidly changing landscape.

Emerging Trends and Upcoming Features

Java's future is shaped by ongoing projects and advancements designed to make the language more efficient, scalable, and versatile. Key projects and technologies like **Project Loom** and **GraalVM** promise to significantly enhance Java's capabilities, especially in high-performance and cloud-native applications.

1. Project Loom

Project Loom aims to improve concurrency in Java by introducing lightweight, user-mode threads called **virtual threads**. This enhancement will allow Java applications to handle many more concurrent tasks without consuming excessive resources, which is especially important for applications that need to handle numerous simultaneous requests, such as web servers or real-time applications.

- **Virtual Threads**: Virtual threads are lightweight threads managed by the JVM rather than the operating system. Unlike traditional threads, they consume fewer resources and have minimal overhead, making it feasible to spawn thousands or even millions of threads.

Example of Virtual Threads in Java:

```java
public class VirtualThreadsExample {

    public static void main(String[] args) throws
InterruptedException {

        var executor =
Executors.newVirtualThreadPerTaskExecutor();

        for (int i = 0; i < 10000; i++) {

            executor.submit(() -> {

                System.out.println("Running in virtual
thread: " + Thread.currentThread().getName());

            });

        }

        executor.shutdown();

    }

}
```

Here, newVirtualThreadPerTaskExecutor() creates an executor service that uses virtual threads, allowing you to run thousands of concurrent tasks without overwhelming system resources.

- **Impact of Project Loom**: Project Loom will make Java more competitive for high-performance, highly concurrent applications, reducing the complexity of asynchronous programming. This could simplify development in areas like real-time applications, microservices, and event-driven architectures by enabling synchronous code to handle asynchronous tasks efficiently.

2. GraalVM

GraalVM is a high-performance runtime that extends the capabilities of the JVM to support multiple languages (e.g., JavaScript, Python, Ruby) and offers significant performance improvements through its native image feature. By compiling Java applications ahead of time to native machine code, GraalVM reduces startup time and memory usage, making it ideal for cloud-native and serverless applications.

- **Native Image**: GraalVM's native image feature allows Java applications to be compiled into standalone executables, resulting in faster startup times and lower memory consumption. This is particularly useful for microservices and serverless environments where application instances are frequently started and stopped.

Example of Creating a Native Image with GraalVM:

bash

```
# Compile Java application to a native image

gu install native-image

native-image -jar myapp.jar
```

By running this command, the Java application is compiled to a native executable, which launches faster and has a smaller footprint than traditional JVM applications.

- **Polyglot Capabilities**: GraalVM enables interoperability between languages, making it possible to use Java with JavaScript, Python, and R in the same application. This feature is valuable for projects that need to combine the strengths of different programming languages in areas like data science and machine learning.

3. Project Panama

Project Panama focuses on improving Java's interoperability with native code, making it easier for Java applications to interact with native libraries written in C, C++, or other languages. This project aims to improve performance and make Java more suitable for use cases that require direct access to hardware or native libraries.

- **Foreign Function and Memory API**: Project Panama introduces the Foreign Function and Memory (FFM) API, which simplifies calling native libraries from Java. It replaces JNI (Java Native Interface) with a safer, more efficient API for working with native code.

Example of Calling Native Code Using FFM API:

```java
import java.foreign.memory.MemorySegment;
import java.foreign.LibraryLookup;

public class NativeExample {
    public static void main(String[] args) {
        var mathLib =
LibraryLookup.ofDefault().lookup("sqrt").get();
        double result = mathLib.apply(16);
        System.out.println("Square root of 16 is: " +
result);
    }
}
```

This example demonstrates how the FFM API can simplify integration with native libraries, which is essential in high-performance computing and IoT.

Java's Evolving Role in Areas Like Blockchain and AI

Java has extended its reach into emerging fields like blockchain and artificial intelligence, thanks to its flexibility, extensive libraries, and strong developer community. Here's how Java is evolving to meet the demands of these rapidly advancing areas.

1. Java in Blockchain Development

Blockchain technology, which powers decentralized applications and cryptocurrencies, has gained significant traction in recent years. Java, with its security features and reliability, is well-suited for blockchain applications.

- **Blockchain Frameworks for Java**: Java developers can leverage frameworks like **Hyperledger Fabric** and **Corda** to create blockchain applications. These frameworks support building secure, distributed ledgers that enable transparent and tamper-proof record keeping.

Example of Using Hyperledger Fabric with Java:

```
import org.hyperledger.fabric.gateway.Wallet;

import org.hyperledger.fabric.gateway.Gateway;

import org.hyperledger.fabric.gateway.Contract;


public class BlockchainExample {

    public static void main(String[] args) throws Exception {
```

```
        Wallet wallet =
Wallet.createFileSystemWallet(Paths.get("wallet"));

        Gateway gateway =
Gateway.createBuilder().identity(wallet,
"user1").connect();

        Contract contract =
gateway.getNetwork("mychannel").getContract("mych
aincode");


        byte[] result =
contract.evaluateTransaction("queryAllAssets");

        System.out.println(new String(result));

    }

}
```

This code demonstrates querying a Hyperledger Fabric network using Java, allowing access to blockchain transactions and records.

- **Smart Contracts**: Java's strong typing and security make it suitable for writing smart contracts. Corda, a blockchain platform specifically designed for regulated industries, provides an SDK that allows developers to write smart contracts in Java, facilitating blockchain solutions in finance, healthcare, and supply chain management.

2. Java in Artificial Intelligence (AI) and Machine Learning

AI and machine learning are transforming industries, and Java has become a viable language for building intelligent applications thanks to new frameworks and interoperability with popular machine learning libraries.

- **Machine Learning Libraries for Java**: Java offers machine learning libraries like **Deep Java Library (DJL)**, **Deeplearning4j (DL4J)**, and **Weka**. These libraries support neural networks, decision trees, and data processing, enabling Java applications to integrate AI features.

Example of Using Deep Java Library (DJL) for Image Classification:

java

```java
import ai.djl.Application;

import ai.djl.Model;

import ai.djl.ModelException;

import ai.djl.inference.Predictor;

import ai.djl.modality.Classifications;

import ai.djl.translate.TranslateException;
```

```java
public class ImageClassifier {

    public static void main(String[] args) throws
ModelException, TranslateException {

        Model model = Model.newInstance("resnet");

        Predictor<Image, Classifications> predictor =
model.newPredictor();


        Image img =
ImageFactory.getInstance().fromUrl("https://path/to/i
mage.jpg");

        Classifications result = predictor.predict(img);


        System.out.println("Prediction: " + result);

    }

}
```

This code performs image classification using DJL,
showcasing how Java applications can integrate deep
learning capabilities.

- **Interoperability with Python for AI**: Java's
  integration with GraalVM enables Java
  applications to run Python code, making it
  easier to access machine learning libraries like
  TensorFlow and PyTorch. This allows Java
  applications to leverage Python's extensive AI
  ecosystem, bringing advanced machine learning

models into production environments that require Java's stability and scalability.

Final Thoughts: Encouraging Readers to Stay Adaptive and Continue Learning

Java has undergone significant evolution since its inception, adapting to meet the demands of modern development environments, cloud computing, IoT, AI, and more. As the technology landscape continues to change, Java developers must stay adaptable and keep up with new developments. Here are some final thoughts on how to continue growing as a Java developer in a rapidly evolving world.

1. Embrace Continuous Learning

Software development is a dynamic field, and Java is constantly advancing with new features, tools, and libraries. Staying updated with industry trends, upcoming JDK releases, and key projects like Project Loom, GraalVM, and Panama is essential to remain competitive and leverage Java's full potential.

- **Read Documentation and RFCs**: Regularly review Java's official documentation, release notes, and JDK enhancement proposals (JEPs) to stay informed about upcoming features.

- **Experiment with New Projects**: Hands-on experimentation with projects like Loom and GraalVM can give developers an edge in understanding how to apply these technologies to real-world problems.

2. Explore Cross-Disciplinary Areas

Java's relevance extends beyond traditional enterprise software. Today, Java developers have the opportunity to work on diverse projects in AI, blockchain, IoT, and edge computing.

- **AI and Machine Learning**: Gain knowledge in machine learning by exploring libraries like DJL or by integrating Java with Python-based ML tools through GraalVM.

- **Blockchain Development**: With Java's security and reliability, blockchain is an exciting area for Java developers, especially in industries like finance and logistics.

3. Leverage Community Resources

Java has one of the largest developer communities, providing ample resources for learning and support. Engaging with the community can help developers stay current and solve problems effectively.

- **Open Source Contributions**: Contributing to open-source Java projects helps developers improve their skills, gain recognition, and stay at the forefront of new developments.

- **Developer Conferences and Meetups**: Java conferences like JavaOne, Devoxx, and local meetups offer a wealth of knowledge and networking opportunities.

4. Focus on Cloud-Native Skills

As cloud computing becomes the dominant mode of deployment, understanding cloud-native development with Java will become increasingly important. Skills like containerization, serverless deployment, and microservices are valuable for modern Java developers.

- **Containerization and Orchestration**: Learn how to package Java applications in Docker containers and manage them with Kubernetes. These skills are essential for deploying and managing scalable applications.

- **Serverless Computing**: Understand serverless architectures by working with AWS Lambda, Azure Functions, or Google Cloud Functions, which support Java applications in a cost-effective, scalable way.

Conclusion

Java's journey has spanned over two decades, and its future looks promising with exciting developments in cloud computing, concurrency, AI, and blockchain. The language's adaptability and commitment to modernization keep it relevant across a wide range of industries and applications. Emerging technologies like Project Loom, GraalVM, and advancements in machine learning libraries continue to shape Java's future, enabling developers to tackle new challenges and build innovative solutions.

By staying adaptable, continuously learning, and exploring cross-disciplinary fields, Java developers can remain at the forefront of technology. Java's robust ecosystem, vast community, and consistent evolution make it a powerful tool for solving the complex challenges of tomorrow. Whether you're venturing into AI, blockchain, or cloud-native development, Java provides the foundation and flexibility to grow along with you on your journey in this ever-evolving field.

Conclusion: Continuing the Journey

As we reach the end of this comprehensive journey through advanced Java programming, it's important to take a moment to reflect on the principles, tools, and best practices that have been explored. From tackling complex system design to mastering high-performance application development, this book has provided you with insights that will serve as valuable resources as you continue to refine your skills and build scalable, resilient applications. Let's recap the core principles covered, discuss actionable tips for applying them in real-world projects, and consider the future of Java in technology with advice on staying up-to-date.

Recap of Core Principles Learned and Their Applications

The topics covered in this book spanned a wide array of essential concepts, from concurrency to security, distributed systems, and beyond. Here's a summary of the core principles and how they apply to building scalable, performant applications in various domains:

1. **Concurrency and Multithreading**: We began with Java's concurrency model and covered essential techniques for managing threads, pools, and asynchronous tasks. Mastering concurrency is vital for building responsive, scalable systems that can handle numerous simultaneous tasks, such as handling multiple client requests on a server, processing data streams in real-time, and supporting parallel processing in machine learning applications.

2. **Memory Management and Optimization**: Efficient memory management allows applications to remain stable and responsive even under high load. Understanding Java's garbage collection strategies and optimizing memory usage through stack and heap management is critical, especially in applications that handle large data volumes, such as data analytics platforms or enterprise resource planning systems.

3. **Advanced Data Structures and Algorithms**: Selecting optimal data structures and implementing algorithmic optimizations can dramatically impact application performance. By choosing the right data structures for tasks such as caching, searching, and sorting, developers can enhance both speed and efficiency. These skills are particularly valuable in applications requiring real-time data access,

like high-frequency trading platforms or interactive web applications.

4. **Dependency Injection and Inversion of Control**: Using dependency injection (DI) and IoC allows for modular, flexible code that is easier to test and scale. This principle is widely used in microservices architecture, where each service is independently testable and deployable, allowing applications to grow without becoming tightly coupled. DI is foundational in frameworks like Spring, which supports the creation of enterprise applications that scale and evolve over time.

5. **Microservices Architecture and Distributed Computing**: Designing applications using microservices and distributed systems principles enables Java developers to create modular, loosely coupled systems that scale horizontally. Microservices facilitate independent development and deployment, allowing each component to be optimized or scaled individually, a necessity in large-scale enterprise applications.

6. **Design Patterns for Scalability**: Applying design patterns like Singleton, Factory, and Observer allows developers to solve common problems efficiently while maintaining flexibility. Design patterns promote clean, modular design that simplifies both

development and maintenance. These patterns are particularly useful in creating maintainable codebases for long-term projects and complex, evolving systems.

7. **Event-Driven and Reactive Programming**: Embracing reactive programming with Java libraries like Project Reactor and RxJava enables developers to create applications that respond dynamically to data and events. This approach is invaluable for building responsive, high-performance applications in IoT, finance, and any real-time data streaming scenarios.

8. **Security Best Practices**: Implementing security principles like data protection, secure API design, and robust authentication mechanisms helps secure applications against cyber threats. Security practices are essential in sectors like e-commerce, finance, and healthcare, where user data protection and secure transaction handling are critical.

9. **Testing and Debugging Strategies**: Rigorous testing through unit, integration, and end-to-end testing ensures applications are reliable and meet quality standards. Debugging techniques covered in this book empower developers to identify and resolve issues early, reducing costly fixes in production. This approach is particularly beneficial in maintaining

applications with high uptime requirements, such as SaaS platforms.

10. **Cloud and Serverless Environments**: Understanding how to deploy Java applications to cloud platforms like AWS, Azure, and GCP, as well as using serverless architecture, is crucial in today's development landscape. Cloud and serverless deployments facilitate scalability, high availability, and resilience, and are especially useful for applications with unpredictable workloads.

Final Tips for Implementing Java Principles in Your Own Projects

Now that you have a strong foundation in advanced Java concepts, here are some practical tips for applying what you've learned:

1. **Start Small and Build Incrementally**: When implementing a complex feature, such as a microservices architecture or a new concurrency model, start with a smaller prototype. Test individual components before

integrating them into the larger system. This will allow you to refine your approach and identify potential issues early.

2. **Prioritize Code Readability and Maintainability**: Code should be written with future maintenance in mind. Use clean coding practices, follow Java naming conventions, and write comprehensive comments. Design patterns and principles like SOLID (Single responsibility, Open-closed, Liskov substitution, Interface segregation, Dependency inversion) will help you maintain a high-quality codebase.

3. **Make Use of Automated Testing**: Implement test-driven development (TDD) wherever feasible to ensure that your code is thoroughly tested from the start. Unit tests should cover individual functions, while integration tests should verify that your components work seamlessly together. Use tools like JUnit, Mockito, and Spring Test to automate testing and maintain code reliability.

4. **Optimize Based on Data**: Avoid premature optimization. Profile your application, using tools like VisualVM or JProfiler, to identify bottlenecks, and optimize only those sections that impact performance. For example, if memory usage is high, focus on optimizing data

structures and garbage collection rather than overhauling the entire system.

5. **Apply Dependency Injection for Flexibility**: Use dependency injection to create loosely coupled components. In larger projects, frameworks like Spring's IoC container make it easier to manage dependencies, allowing for a flexible and maintainable architecture.

6. **Utilize Version Control and CI/CD Pipelines**: Use Git for version control and set up continuous integration and deployment (CI/CD) pipelines with tools like Jenkins, GitLab CI, or GitHub Actions. Automated pipelines streamline testing and deployment, ensuring consistent, error-free updates.

7. **Document and Share Your Knowledge**: Documentation is vital for team collaboration and knowledge sharing. Create detailed documentation on your application's design, dependencies, and testing processes. Additionally, contribute to community forums or write about your experiences—sharing knowledge strengthens your understanding and benefits others.

Future Outlook on Java's Place in Tech and Advice for Staying Up-to-Date

Java's consistent evolution and adaptability to new technologies have cemented its place in the tech industry for decades, and its future remains bright. With advancements like **Project Loom, GraalVM,** and **Project Panama**, Java is well-positioned to maintain its relevance in fields like cloud computing, big data, artificial intelligence, and more. Here are some key areas where Java is poised to continue its impact, along with advice for staying current with Java's developments.

1. Expanding Use in Cloud-Native and Microservices Architectures

Java's robust frameworks, like Spring Boot and Micronaut, are extensively used in developing cloud-native and microservices applications. As cloud adoption continues to grow, Java developers skilled in cloud-native practices, serverless architectures, and containerization will be highly sought after. Embrace tools like Kubernetes for container orchestration and GraalVM's native image compilation to deploy efficient, fast-starting Java applications in cloud environments.

2. Java in High-Concurrency Applications with Project Loom

Project Loom's virtual threads will soon transform how Java handles concurrency, allowing developers to write synchronous code that can handle asynchronous workloads efficiently. This will simplify the development of applications requiring high concurrency, such as real-time gaming, financial trading platforms, and data analytics. Following the development of Project Loom and experimenting with its capabilities in your projects will prepare you for future high-demand applications.

3. The Role of Java in Machine Learning and AI

Java's ecosystem has expanded to include libraries like Deep Java Library (DJL) and Deeplearning4j, which allow for machine learning and deep learning applications. With support for multi-language interoperability via GraalVM, Java can integrate with popular ML libraries from other languages like Python, bridging the gap between Java and AI-heavy applications. For developers interested in AI, gaining experience with Java-based machine learning libraries and exploring GraalVM's polyglot capabilities will be beneficial.

4. Adoption in Blockchain and Distributed Ledger Technology

As blockchain gains traction in finance, supply chain, and healthcare, Java's security and reliability make it well-suited for developing blockchain applications. Frameworks like Hyperledger Fabric and Corda enable Java developers to create decentralized applications and smart contracts. Java developers interested in blockchain can explore these frameworks to become proficient in building secure, distributed applications.

5. Staying Up-to-Date with Java

Keeping up with Java's evolving features and tools is essential. Here are some strategies for staying current:

- **Follow JDK Release Notes and JEPs**: Each Java Development Kit (JDK) release introduces new features and improvements. Review the release notes and Java Enhancement Proposals (JEPs) to understand how these changes can impact your work.

- **Experiment with New Features**: Hands-on experience with new Java features, such as virtual threads from Project Loom or native images from GraalVM, will deepen your understanding and make you more competitive as a developer.

- **Engage with the Java Community**: Attending Java conferences like JavaOne, Devoxx, and JAX provides insights into the latest trends and networking opportunities. Joining forums like Stack Overflow, Reddit's r/java, or the Java community on Twitter can also keep you informed about the latest tools, practices, and project updates.

- **Expand Beyond Core Java**: Java's applicability extends to frameworks like Spring,

Hibernate, and Micronaut, and platforms like Kubernetes and AWS. Expanding your expertise into these areas broadens your capabilities and positions you well for diverse roles in tech.

Final Words

As you embark on the next stage of your Java programming journey, remember that learning is a continuous process. The principles and techniques you've acquired provide a foundation, but ongoing practice, experimentation, and adaptation to new advancements are essential to mastering any technology. Java's place in the industry remains strong, and as you develop your skills further, you'll find endless opportunities to apply them in impactful, innovative ways.

Stay curious, keep challenging yourself, and always look for ways to deepen your knowledge. The tech landscape will continue to evolve, and by embracing this mindset, you'll not only keep pace but thrive.